Founder and Contributing Editor:
  Lyndon H. LaRouche, Jr.
Editorial Board: *Lyndon H. LaRouche, Jr.,*
  Antony Papert, Gerald Rose, Dennis Small,
  Nancy Spannaus, Jeffrey Steinberg, William
  Wertz
Editor: *Nancy Spannaus*
Managing Editors: *Bonnie James, Susan Welsh*
Technology Editor: *Marsha Freeman*
Book Editor: *Katherine Notley*
Graphics Editor: *Alan Yue*
Photo Editor: *Stuart Lewis*
Circulation Manager: *Stanley Ezrol*

INTELLIGENCE DIRECTORS
Counterintelligence: *Jeffrey Steinberg, Michele*
  Steinberg
Economics: *John Hoefle, Marcia Merry Baker,*
  Paul Gallagher
History: *Anton Chaitkin*
Ibero-America: *Dennis Small*
Russia and Eastern Europe: *Rachel Douglas*
United States: *Debra Freeman*

INTERNATIONAL BUREAUS
Bogotá: *Javier Almario*
Berlin: *Rainer Apel*
Copenhagen: *Tom Gillesberg*
Houston: *Harley Schlanger*
Lima: *Sara Madueño*
Melbourne: *Robert Barwick*
Mexico City: *Gerardo Castilleja Chávez*
New Delhi: *Ramtanu Maitra*
Paris: *Christine Bierre*
Stockholm: *Ulf Sandmark*
United Nations, N.Y.C.: *Leni Rubinstein*
Washington, D.C.: *William Jones*
Wiesbaden: *Göran Haglund*

ON THE WEB
e-mail: eirns@larouchepub.com
www.larouchepub.com
www.executiveintelligencereview.com
www.larouchepub.com/eiw
Webmaster: *John Sigerson*
Assistant Webmaster: *George Hollis*
Editor, Arabic-language edition: *Hussein Askary*

EIR (ISSN 0273-6314) *is published weekly*
(50 issues), by EIR News Service, Inc.,
P.O. Box 17390, Washington, D.C. 20041-0390.
(703) 777-9451

European Headquarters: E.I.R. GmbH, Postfach
Bahnstrasse 9a, D-65205, Wiesbaden, Germany
Tel: 49-611-73650
Homepage: http://www.eirna.com
e-mail: eirna@eirna.com
Director: Georg Neudecker

Montreal, Canada: 514-461-1557

Denmark: EIR - Danmark, Sankt Knuds Vej 11,
basement left, DK-1903 Frederiksberg, Denmark.
Tel.: +45 35 43 60 40, Fax: +45 35 43 87 57. e-mail:
eirdk@hotmail.com.

Mexico City: EIR , Calz de los Gallos 39 interior 2,
Col Plutarco E Calles,
Del. Miguel Hidalgo, CP 11350,
Mexico, DF. Tel 5318-2301, 6306-8363, 6306-8361

Canada Post Publication Sales Agreement
#40683579

Postmaster: Send all address changes to *EIR*, P.O.
Box 17390, Washington, D.C. 20041-0390.

From the Editors

Our first issue of 2015 looks forward to our adopted mission for this year: Defeating the British Empire and bringing the United States and Western Europe into collaboration with the BRICS.

This mission is coherent with two major anniversaries that the world will celebrate this year. First, the United States' victory over the British Empire and its Confederacy in 1865—which led to the takeoff of U.S. industrial might, and the spread of its model throughout the world. Anton Chaitkin's *History* feature in this issue, on the battle in the 1870s U.S., brings this period to life in a way that should inspire you about what can be done today.

The world this year also celebrates the 70th anniversary of the Allied victory over Fascism, even as the globe is threatened by a fascist upsurge once again. Russia and China, in particular, are commemorating this event with great emotion, as they face new aggression from the West. Will sane forces in the West reject this resurgence of evil in time?

The hope lies in the BRICS dynamic, which our *Feature* identifies as of year-beginning, with a necessarily small snapshot of the dramatic process that is upending power relations over the entire planet, and creating the promise of a better life for billions. As we have over the last six months, we will be focusing heavily on publicizing the BRICS developments, and on the political motion in their support, which have been subject to unconscionable blackout by the "major" news media.

We feature coverage of the war front with Russia in our *International* section, providing an inside view seldom available to English-speaking readers, of Russia's preparations to defend itself, both militarily and economically. This view includes our report on a recent event at Dubna University, which was keynoted by Lyndon and Helga LaRouche by video. The transcripts of their well-received messages are included.

Under *Economics*, we lead with the imminent threat of a Wall Street blowout, likely to be detonated by the crashing oil price. All the more urgent that Glass-Steagall be put into effect beforehand, so that Wall Street speculators are the ones damaged, not "Main Street." Then we can get on with investing in the science mankind needs, including in the food supply. The prerequisites for that are outlined in an interview with the 2014 World Food Prize winner, Sanjaya Rajaram, done by our Mexican colleagues. Don't miss it.

EIR Contents

Xinhua/Liu Weibing

2015; Join the BRICS, or Face Wall St. Crash & War

by the Editors

Dec. 29—A new system of economic and strategic relations among sovereign nations, centered on the BRICS (Brazil, Russia, India, China, South Africa) and their allies in South America, Asia, and Africa, is poised to dominate the world in 2015. This new arrangement, representing more than half of humanity, holds the promise of freeing the globe from the barbarous stranglehold of the British Empire, and its satrapies, including Saudi Arabia, Wall Street, and the current Presidency of the United States.

"The truth of the matter is, the greatest margin of political power in the world lies in the hands of the BRICS body and its associates," noted Lyndon LaRouche Dec. 28.

Over the past six months, highlighted by the July Fortaleza, Brazil Summit, the BRICS nations have forged ahead to establish a new set of international agreements for both economic and military security, with an increasingly open self-confidence in their role. Crucial to these agreements has been an emphasis on both basic economic infrastructure, and cooperation on the frontiers of scientific endeavor, especially space and nuclear energy. The latter, as stressed by economist LaRouche, is the keystone for success.

In year-end statements, the governments of Russia, China, and Brazil put forward their perspectives for 2015, in a manner that makes clear their world-historical self-conception, as a counterpole to the current system of geopolitical conflict and economic collapse, as you will see below.

Russia: BRICS To Set the Agenda

On Dec. 27, a statement by the Russian Foreign Ministry on the prospects for 2015 elaborated on the global context in which the government sees its initiatives for the year, including the Eurasian Economic Union (EEU). Moscow has prioritized "efforts to transform the BRICS into one of the most important elements of the system of global governance" as part of a major foreign policy impetus, said the statement.

"Crucial progress towards this goal has been made during the Fortaleza Summit (July 15-16)—the decision to establish a multilateral framework of the association of financial institutions—a New Development Bank and a contingent of foreign exchange reserves with a total resource of $200 billion," it said. BRICS leaders, who met on the sidelines of a G20 summit in November, have instructed their finance ministers to name the new bank's president by the time they next meet in Russia.

In July 2015, the BRICS and the Shanghai Cooperation Organization (SCO), both then under Russian chairmanship, will hold back-to-back summits in Ufa, the capital of Russia's Republic of Bashkortostan.

Russia has spoken "with one voice with its partners in the BRICS for the promotion of international stability in its various dimensions," said the Foreign Ministry statement. The Fortaleza Summit condemned "unilateral military intervention and economic sanctions," the statement noted.

On Jan. 1, 2015, the EEU will begin operation, with

共和国主席习近平对巴西
6 a 18 de ju... 2014 ...

Agência Brasil/Marcelo Camargo

Xinhua

Russian Presidential Press and Information Service

2014 saw the breakout of the BRICS nations, with more to come in 2015. Right: Russian President Vladimir Putin and Indian Prime Minister Narendra Modi at the BRICS summit, July 2014; above, a Chinese rocket carrying the CBERS-4 satellite, jointly developed with Brazil, blasts off in Taiyuahn, China; top right, Brazilian President Dilma Rousseff welcomes Chinese President Xi Jinping to the Fortaleza Summit.

the aim of conducting "a coordinated policy in key economic areas such as energy, industry, agriculture, and transport" among a core group of five nations—Belarus, Kazakhstan, Russia, Armenia, and Kyrgyzstan. The EEU will have three components, with the headquarters in Moscow, the court in Belarus, and the financial institution in Kazakhstan.

At the finalizing meeting of Presidents of the EEU nations on Dec. 23, Russian President Vladimir Putin stressed the benefits of the union for all the nations involved, and that the institution is open to other nations to integrate economically based on mutual benefit. Already, the EEU is in negotiations with South America's

Mercosur (Common Market of the South), Turkey, India, Israel, and the Association of Southeast Asian Nations (ASEAN) for cooperation agreements.

In their summit last May in Shanghai, President Putin and Chinese President Xi Jinping agreed on the perspective of cooperation between the EEU and the Chinese Silk Road Economic Belt, especially for creating a new Eurasian transportation grid.

China: A 'Win-Win' Vision

Chinese Foreign Minister Wang Yi made his government's official statement of policy at a Dec. 24 symposium sponsored by the China Institute of International Studies and the China Foundation for International Studies. He began by summarizing China's accomplishments during 2014, which he sees being extended into "building a global network of partnerships" during the coming year.

China has "promoted the Chinese vision of building a new type of international relations," with "win-win cooperation at its heart," Wang said. "As a new approach to managing state-to-state relations in the contemporary world, it will exert a positive and profound impact on the evolution of international relations."

Wang described China's approach of forming partners instead of allies, in some detail, noting that "China has established 72 partnerships in different forms and at different levels with 67 countries and 5 regions or regional organizations, which cover all the major countries and regions in the world.

"The partnerships that we are building have three basic features. First, equality. Countries, regardless of their size or level of development, should respect each other's sovereignty, independence, and territorial integrity, as well as each other's choice of development path and values, treat each other as equals, and show mutual understanding and support for each other.

"Second, peace. What makes such partnership different from military alliance is that it does not have any hypothetical enemy nor is it targeted at any third party, thus keeping relations between countries unaffected by military factors. It aims to handle state-to-state relations with a cooperative rather than confrontational, and a win-win rather than zero-sum approach.

"Third, inclusiveness. The partnership we have initiated seeks to go beyond differences in social systems and ideologies to maximize interests and pursue a common goal."

Wang pointed to the Silk Road Economic Belt and the 21st Century Maritime Silk Road, projects launched in 2014, as examples of such partnerships. He also underlined President Xi Jingping's call for an "Asia-Pacific Dream" at the November 2014 APEC conference, and a new security architecture, which he introduced at this year's Conference on Interaction and Confidence-Building Measures. "China has used the CICA [Conference on Interaction and Confidence Building in Asia] platform to champion security cooperation by rejecting the old mentality of seeking one's own security at the expense of the security of others, and building an open and inclusive new security architecture in Asia. This shows China's eagerness to take a more constructive part in Asia's security affairs and provide public security goods," Wang said.

Wang discussed the extraordinary diplomatic activity by President Xi and Prime Minister Li Keqiang during the year—including meeting with over 500 foreign leaders while creating the Asia Infrastructure Investment Bank (AIIB) and the BRICS' New Development Bank (NDB). He characterized the principles of China's foreign policy as the following: 1) Upholding the social system and development path chosen by China and supported overwhelmingly by the Chinese people; 2) pursuing peace and non-interference in the internal affairs of other countries; 3) promoting justice in an even-handed way; and 4) making domestic development and reform, and opening up, top priorities.

Wang concluded with an appeal to his audience to continue on the path laid out by President Xi and the party leadership, and to realize "the glorious mission history has bestowed on this generation of ours."

Brazil: 'We Acted'

The Foreign Ministry of Brazil also issued a year-end statement of note on the BRICS perspective.

Flavio Damico, director of the Inter-Region Mechanisms Department, told Xinhua-Spanish on Dec. 17 that the BRICS nations' decision to found the New Development Bank and a Contingency Reverse Arrangement to protect their currencies, epitomizes the transformation which the BRICS made in 2014. The countries went beyond "discussing the world order, to 'offering a global public good' which will support the process of development in the emerging world. *Instead of talking, we acted* [emphasis added].

"That is the fundamental change. That is the great task of the BRICS from here on out: to carry out the process of institutionalization, establishing those two major institutions," he said, referring to the new bank and the currency agreement, which are not yet operational.

Damico reported that the BRICS set deadlines for implementation of their program at their meeting on the sidelines of the G20 Summit in Brisbane, Australia, in November 2014, with the goal of producing concrete results by the July 2015 BRICS summit. For one, the respective national Congresses are to ratify the creation of the bank within a year, while an interim committee carries out the preparatory work.

Between now and April, when Brazil hands the role of *pro tempore* head of the BRICS over to Russia, there are additional meetings scheduled, including one of the BRICS Ministers of Science and Technology, of Agriculture, and of Education, and a meeting on "populations."

"We are going to go ahead with discussion of a long-term project to strengthen economic cooperation among the BRICS. This should basically be measures to facilitate trade and investment among the five countries," he added.

Progress Underway

The lack of final formal arrangements on the two financial institutions the BRICS are planning, is not holding back progress on closer collaboration. Not a week goes by without the announcement of new agreements both on physical projects, and on currency arrangements to pay for them, among the BRICS nations and their partners. A review of just the last two weeks of December turns up the following items, which are by no means exhaustive.

• China-Egypt: On Dec. 23, Egyptian President Abdel Fattah el-Sisi began a four-day trip to China, with the declared intent of making Egypt "a mainstay in the initiative of Chinese President Xi Jinping to revive the ancient Chinese Silk Road trade route." El-Sisi mentioned that the new Suez Canal Development Project, which Egypt is financing itself on a crash-project basis, will be a key part of the Silk Road Initiative.

The two nations signed 25 agreements, mainly in energy and transportation, including plans for construction of a high-speed train to connect Alexandria, on the Mediterranean coast, with Aswan, in the South; an electric railway network in the densely populated Cairo-Nile Delta region; and Egypt's first nuclear power plant.

• India-Russia: On Dec. 24, the head of the Crimean administration, Sergei Aksyonov, said: "We have reached an agreement with the Indian side that we will jointly build a pharmaceutical plant."

• Rusia-Brazil: On Dec. 18, Russian Deputy Prime Minister Dmitri Rogozin visited Brazil's science center in São José dos Campos, and discussed joint work on space launches and other advanced scientific areas: "In a word, we may establish a long-term firendship with Brazil in the area of high technologies," Rogozin said.

• Russia-Argentina-Spain: On Dec. 19, Argentina's Planning and Foreign Ministers announced that a Spanish-Argentine consortium, plus Russia's Inter RAO Export firm, had won the contract to build the Chihuido I hydroelectric plant in Argentina, at a cost of $2.1 billion.

• China-Thailand: Chinese Premier Li attended the triennial meeting of the Greater Mekong Subregion on Dec. 20, where a 10-year development plan valued at over $50 billion was proposed, to be comprised primarily of projects in infrastructure and transportation. The Mekong River Basin water project, which has been sabotaged by the anti-human "environmentalist" policy of the World Bank and Asian Development Bank for decades, would be a crucial boost for upgrading the economies of the six nations in this region—Cambodia, China, Laos, Myanmar, Thailand, and Vietnam.

• China-Eastern Europe: Prime Minister Li, during the second week of December, attended the fourth annual Belgrade Economic Forum of the heads of state and government of 16 Central and Eastern European States—of which he has been made a member. Fourteen heads of state attended this meeting, at which infrastructure, stretching north from Greece's port of Piraeus, was on the agenda. According to the Greek paper *Kathimerini* (ekathimerini.com), the project underway to expand the port is now a Maritime Silk Road catalyst for an Athens to Belgrade to Central Europe project (Athens being reconnected with Piraeus by rail).

A Casus Belli?

None of the BRICS nations, nor most of their allies, are under any illusion that their plans for development will proceed unimpeded. Indeed, the leading political representatives of the bankrupt Western nations—especially the United States and the European Union—have constantly deployed to sabotage the consolidation of what they cannot fail to see as an economic superpower, coming together within the BRICS alliance.

Indeed, in LaRouche's view, the British-Wall Street crowd, who are staring their own bankruptcy in the face, have determined that they are prepared to provoke all-out war, if necessary, in order to crush the BRICS alliance, despite the fact that BRICS leaders such as China and Russia have repeatedly extended offers of collaboration to the United States and the EU countries.

Thus, the pathway ahead in 2015 is a choice between two starkly different alternatives: on the one side, a financial and economic collapse worse than any in history, leading directly into global warfare that threatens mankind's existence on the planet; and on the other, an unprecedented era of collaboration among sovereign nations for economic progress on the highest level.

Is there really a choice?

The New Silk Road Becomes The World Land-Bridge

The BRICS countries have a strategy to prevent war and economic catastrophe. It's time for the rest of the world to join!

This 374-page report is a road-map to the New World Economic Order that Lyndon and Helga LaRouche have championed for over 20 years. This path is currently being charted by the nations of the BRICS (Brazil, Russia, India, China, and South Africa), which are leading a dynamic of global optimism toward real economic development, complete with new credit institutions and major high-technology projects for uplifting all mankind.

Includes:

Introduction by Helga Zepp-LaRouche, "The New Silk Road Leads to the Future of Mankind!"

The metrics of progress, with emphasis on the scientific principles required for survival of mankind: nuclear power and desalination; the fusion power economy; solving the water crisis. Detailed maps show what has been accomplished and what has not, since Zepp-LaRouche first addressed a Beijing conference on the Eurasian Land-Bridge in 1996.

The three keystone nations: China, the core nation of the New Silk Road; Russia's mission in North Central Eurasia and the Arctic; India prepares to take on its legacy of leadership.

Other Regions: The potential contributions of Southwest, Central, and Southeast Asia; Australia as a driver for Pacific Development; Europe, the western pole of the New Silk Road; Africa—the Test for Global Progress; bringing the Western Hemisphere on board; the LaRouches' 40-year fight for international development.

BRITISH AND OBAMA WAGE FINANCIAL WARFARE

Economic Assault on Russia Raises Threat of World War

by Rachel Douglas

Dec. 29—Representatives of the City of London and Wall Street, which are more bankrupt than ever and stand to lose their power forever, if the United States and Europe join with the BRICS and opt for a future of real economic development, closed out 2014 with manic outbursts about overthrowing Russian President Vladimir Putin. On Dec. 16, Lyndon LaRouche blasted these British circles, and President Barack Obama, for bringing the world to the brink of general war, by economic warfare against Russia with the political and strategic goal of regime-change. "These are not economic measures," LaRouche said of recent months' oil-price pressure and trade sanctions against Russia, "These are acts of war and will be seen as such in Moscow."

Russian officials already leave no doubt, that they see the year-end attacks on the ruble as part of a regime-change drive that will not be tolerated. Former Prime Minister Mikhail Fradkov, current head of the Foreign Intelligence Service (SVR), so warned on Dec. 5, ten days before the Black Monday (Dec. 15) crash of the Russian currency by 12% in one day. Asked by Bloomberg about Western intentions to oust Putin, Fradkov said, "Such a desire has been noticed, it's a small secret. No one wants to see a strong and independent Russia." He attributed the more than 30% drop in oil prices partly to U.S. actions, adding that foreign investment funds were "taking part in ruble speculation via intermediaries." Foreign Minister Sergei Lavrov, questioned by France 24 TV in a Dec. 16 interview as to whether sanc-

tions were "a way of trying to create a regime-change in Russia," was succinct and to the point: "I have very serious reasons to believe that this is the case."

Lavrov's "serious reasons" surely include the overt statements of top American and British officials. Obama has boasted of his intention to outplay Putin in a high-stakes geopolitical game. "Putin does not have good cards," the U.S. President told the White House Export Council on Dec. 11, "and he has not played them as well as the Western press seems to give him credit for. Putin will succeed if he creates a rift in the trans-Atlantic relationship, if we see Europe divided from the United States. That would be a strategic victory for him and I intend on preventing that." (Obama was alluding to alarm in Europe at the ever-escalating U.S.-NATO confrontation with Russia.) British Chancellor of the Exchequer George Osborne, addressing the Economic Club of New York in mid-December, gloated that the fall of oil prices "puts a lot more pressure on Vladimir Putin. People had been asking whether sanctions are working, [and] can Putin ride this out.... I don't think that looks so clear now. The Russian budget is heavily dependent on high oil prices. He might be exposed by this."

Washington sources confirm that Saudi Arabia is prepared to continue to over-produce, creating an estimated 1.5- to 2-million-barrel-a-day oil glut, relative to current global requirements, and thus to keep prices low until many rivals in the oil and natural gas markets are bankrupted.

The media chimed in, focusing less on the prospects for serious unrest against the popular Russian President, than on a fresh-baked scenario for "Putin to be replaced in a palace coup," as *Time* magazine fantasized on Dec. 15. "Will Russian Ruble Collapse Trigger a Military Coup against Vladimir Putin?" (*International Business Times*, Dec. 16). "Russia: Why Oil Crash Could Threaten Vladimir Putin with a Palace Coup" (*The Guardian*, Dec. 17). "Putin Could Be Finished" (*The Hill*, Dec. 13).

A journalist for Reuters, which has a long and intimate history with British Intelligence, brought the ominous coup scenario to Putin's own year-end press conference on Dec. 18, demanding, "To what extent are you confident that your inner circle unconditionally supports you? Do you see any risk of a government coup or even a palace coup? You have stated on a number of occasions what you would do in case of an 'orange revolution' or, God forbid, a 'red revolution.' But do you have a plan in the event of treachery in your inner circle or a palace coup?"

The coordinated "coup" publicity smacked of a cover story for an assassination attempt. Putin handled the press-conference challenge in his own way, with jokes. But readers who may have swallowed the story of an authoritarian Russian leader who invaded Ukraine, threatened other neighboring countries, and thus brought the West's sanctions down on his country, would do well to take it seriously, in light of the following matters. First, what the Russian military *is* doing

Russian leaders are making clear that they view the financial warfare against their country as a threat that could lead to general war, and they are upping their military capabilities accordingly. Left: President Putin visits the anti-submarine ship Vice Admiral Kulakov; below: the Alexander Nevsky, a Borey-class submarine, is assembled at the Sevmash shiphard.

now (as opposed to coup-plotting), in response to the West's growing pressure against Russia; that is the subject of the next section of this article. Second, the coup that really did take place in 2014—in Ukraine. That was the one where the U.S. State Department, and British and EU officials, backed the ouster of an elected President, by a violent, partially NATO-trained paramilitary force espousing a neo-Nazi ideology, as documented in two *EIR* dossiers of the past year.[1]

Putin summarized the view from Moscow of the es-

---

1. "Western Powers Back Neo-Nazi Coup in Ukraine," *EIR*, Feb. 7, 2014; "British Imperial Project in Ukraine: Violent Coup, Fascist Axioms, Neo-Nazis, *EIR*, May 16, 2014.

calating confrontation Dec. 4. in his annual Presidential Address to the Federal Assembly: "The sanctions are not just a knee-jerk reaction on behalf of the United States or its allies to our position regarding the events and the coup in Ukraine, or even the so-called Crimean Spring. I'm sure that if these events had never happened, ... they would have come up with some other excuse to try to contain Russia's growing capabilities, affect our country in some way, or even exploit it for their own purposes."

Global Strategic Threats

On Dec. 26, Putin signed a new edition of Russia's military doctrine. Its core is unchanged from the document adopted in 1999:[2] The doctrine states that the Russian military remains a defensive tool, to be used only as a last resort, and that the purpose of its nuclear forces is to deter potential enemies from attacking Russia, while leaving open the possibility of using them to protect itself from a military attack, either nuclear or conventional, that threatens the country's existence.

This latest periodic update to the doctrine identifies NATO's overall build-up and its eastward expansion as the main external threat to Russia. The U.S./NATO effort to construct a global missile defense system, and the U.S. implementation of its Prompt Global Strike doctrine (including the use of high-precision, non-nuclear weapons), are termed global strategic threats, as senior Russian officers have continuously emphasized in recent years.[3] The document's strategic overview also cites the emergence of new security threats in northern Africa, Syria, Iraq, and Afghanistan, the lack of effective international cooperation against terrorism and the drug trade, and the increased use of private military companies, especially in areas adjacent to Russian borders.

On the domestic front, the revised military doctrine treats regime-change schemes as a form of irregular warfare.[4] It cites threats from "actions aimed at violent change of the constitutional order of the Russian Federation, destabilization of the political and social situation in the country, and disorganization of the functioning of government agencies, and key state, military, and information infrastructure," as well as from "actions by terrorist organizations and individuals, aimed to undermine the sovereignty and violate the unity and territorial integrity of the RF"; "informational" encouragement for Russian youth to reject the traditions of patriotic defense of their homeland; and the provocation of ethnic and social tension.

The revised military doctrine also underscores the military-strategic dimension of the BRICS developments in 2014, citing Russia's cooperation with such organizations as the Shanghai Cooperation Organization (SCO) and the BRICS as important for international security. Deputy Minister of Defense Anatoli Antonov, in his Dec. 24 year-end press conference, said, "We have been using the regional platforms of the Asia-Pacific Region for advancing ideas on creating a new architecture of security and cooperation. Our opinion is being listened to."

Antonov elaborated on the current strategic dangers. "Under the slogan of a Russian threat," he charged, "NATO is building its military potential in the Baltic States, Poland, Bulgaria, and Romania." The state news agency Itar-TASS cited Antonov on NATO's build-up of the number of tanks in Europe and the "more than doubled" number of flights by NATO tactical aircraft along Russian borders in 2014. Russian media played up Antonov's complaint that NATO is training flight crews to handle planes carrying nuclear weapons. "Of particular concern," he was quoted on the Ministry of Defense website, "is the ongoing training of flight crews from non-nuclear NATO members, on nuclear-capable aircraft, and the inclusion of additional countries, such as Poland, in this process."

Having suspended military cooperation with Russia, Antonov said, NATO was trying to turn Ukraine into a "forward line of confrontation with Russia." On Dec. 23, the Ukrainian Parliament had voted to repeal the country's non-aligned status, thereby ratifying the Kiev regime's quest for membership in NATO.

Major advances in Russian strategic military systems were also showcased, as the year drew to a close. On Dec. 26, the Defense Ministry announced the successful test-firing of a road-mobile RS-24 Yars (NATO designation SS-27 mod 2) heavy intercontinental ballistic missile (ICBM) from Plesetsk in northwest

---

2. Rachel Douglas, "Russian 'Doctrine': The Posture of a Big Military Power, Under Attack," *EIR*, Oct. 29, 1999.

3. Carl Osgood, "Russians Reiterate Warning: NATO Faces Preemptive Strike," *EIR*, May 11, 2012; Carl Osgood, Rachel Douglas, "U.S. Moves Toward Nuclear First Strike Capability," *EIR*, March 15, 2013.

4. Tony Papert, "Moscow Conference Identifies 'Color Revolutions' as War," *EIR*, June 13, 2014, reported on the similar discussion by senior Russian military figures, at the May 23 Third Moscow Conference on International Security. The nature of color revolutions as an irregular-warfare instrument of regime-change was the subject of the lead article in the Russian Defense Ministry journal *Voyennaya Mysl* (*Military Thought*) of September 2014.

Russia, with the dummy warheads striking their targets in the Kura test range on Kamchatka Peninsula in the Far East. Also announced by military sources, through Russian wire services, was progress on developing the rail-mobile Barguzin ICBM system, also for Yars-class missiles; its trains will carry six missiles each, with a strategic missile division consisting of five such trains. Commander of the Strategic Missile Forces Gen. Sergei Karakayev announced that a missile called the RS-26 Rubezh, which has been described as a Yars-based smaller ICBM or an IRBM, and as being expressly designed for use against the European BMD program, will go into service in 2016.

Deputy Prime Minister Dmitri Rogozin attended the Dec. 26 keel-laying of the sixth Borey-class ballistic missile submarine, at the Sevmash shipyard in Severodvinsk. He hailed the shipbuilders' contribution "to the defense capability of our country at a crucial moment, when there are attempts to stop us, weaken us with outside pressure and sanctions, and blackmail us, just when Russia is reacquiring its historic image and restoring its territorial integrity, pride and sovereignty." Three Borey-class subs, capable of carrying 16 Bulava submarine-launched ballistic missiles (SLBMs) with multiple warheads, are already in service with the Northern Fleet of the Russian Navy, while a total of three more are now under construction. Construction of the seventh and eighth Borey-class subs will begin in 2015, along with three Yasen-class attack submarines.

Putin took stock of these programs at a Dec. 20 meeting of the Defense Ministry Board, where he said: "Russia will always act consistently to protect its interests and sovereignty and will strive to strengthen international stability and to support equal security for all countries and peoples. At the same time, the situation in the world around us is not becoming any simpler. You all know about the USA's plans to build a missile defense system. NATO has stepped up its activity too, including in Europe, especially in Eastern Europe." Reviewing the requirements of Russia's military doctrine, Putin emphasized the development of strategic weapons, saying, "We must develop all components of our strategic nuclear forces, which play a very important part in maintaining global balance and essentially rule out the possibility of a large-scale attack against Russia. In 2015, the strategic nuclear forces will receive more than 50 intercontinental ballistic missiles."

Financial Warfare

As if oblivious to Russia's status as a nuclear superpower with a formidable array of BRICS and other allies, U.S. Council of Economic Advisors head Jason Furman on Dec. 17 smirked about the ruble's plunge: "I would be extremely concerned if I were President Putin's economic advisor. They are between a rock and a hard place." The Administration had just announced that Obama would sign the Ukraine Freedom Support Act, which authorizes increased sanctions against Russia and lethal military aid for Ukraine.

The Russian currency's Black Monday drop brought its losses to nearly 50% during 2014, closing in the vicinity of 80 rubles to the euro and 65 to the dollar; the ruble had been at around 30 to the dollar for several years, until mid-2014. The immediate factors were low oil prices, the speculators cited by Fradkov, and, as Putin confirmed in his Dec. 18 press conference, "our own companies" selling rubles for dollars. These latter operations are driven in part by the tight-money policy of Russia's Finance Ministry and Central Bank (CBR), a legacy of the monetarist takeover of the country in the 1990s. With borrowing rates inside Russia remaining high, even after the 2008 crisis, state-owned and privatized Russian corporations continued to borrow abroad, at lower rates and in foreign currency, to a total of over $600 billion. Cut off by the sanctions from the ability to roll over these loans, Russian firms sell rubles to obtain foreign currency for debt payments.

The ruble sank to even greater depths on Dec. 16, but rebounded in the days that followed. Putin reported that he had phoned some major CEOs, known as Russia's "oligarchs" from the 1990s privatization process, urging them not to dump the ruble. On Dec. 19, he held a meeting with three dozen of these top "business community" figures. Little of their discussion was made public, but Russian financial press reports indicated, and Central Bank announcements confirm, that the large companies are being offered preferential interest rates and protection from margin calls on (domestic) loans collateralized by the now-devalued shares of their companies, while the CBR also moves to bail out the Russian banks holding such loans.[5]

The CBR's main move was a drastic interest-rate increase: a hike of its benchmark rate by 6.5 percentage points to 17%, announced after midnight on Dec. 16. Despite promises of subsidized exceptions for qualified

---

5. John Helmer, "Dances with Bears" blog post, Dec. 23, 2014.

projects, an outcry against the Central Bank followed, from smaller businesses and even from within the government. "In effect, this means a ban on lending," one Moscow economist put it. Speakers at a Dec. 9 session of the Moscow Economic Forum pointed out that the CBR's high-rates policy, even before the Dec. 16 rate hike, undercut Putin's own call for measures to boost Russian small and medium-sized businesses so they can produce for "import substitution," in the face of the sanctions and the plunging ruble. Rogozin wrote on his Facebook page, Dec. 17, that the 17% rate would be an insurmountable obstacle to industrial development, adding, "I have long demanded that the Ministry of Finance and the Bank of Russia should establish special rules for financing industries under state defense contract programs."

Capital and Exchange Controls?

The most promising responses to the currency warfare against Russia came at the level of the BRICS. A series of articles in official Chinese newspapers, bolstered by statements from the Foreign Ministry, said that China stands ready to help. "We believe that Russia is capable of surmounting the current temporary difficulty," said Foreign Ministry spokesman Qin Gang on Dec. 18, citing the capabilities of the SCO to "safeguard regional security and stability, but also [as] an important platform for all members to pursue common development." Currency and credit swaps arrangements, formalized by Russia and China in October to finance trade in their national currencies, are going into operation and "are not affected by the depreciation of the ruble," Qin said. Emphasizing real-economy cooperation above all, he noted that China's Silk Road Fund will soon be operational and will consider projects in Russia, inclusively.

In Russia itself, there is discussion of more robust ways to defend and advance the national economy, pointing in the direction of what LaRouche, in his Dec. 16 remarks, proposed for counteracting the British-Obama financial provocations. First, LaRouche said, Russia should, without delay, impose capital controls, exchange controls, and other protective measures against the assault of currency speculators. This could be called the "Mahathir solution," after the measures adopted by Malaysia's Prime Minister in 1997.

LaRouche emphasized that Russia and the world need a Hamiltonian credit system to defeat the power of the City of London-Wall Street oligarchy. "If Russia does not take these measures immediately, we are headed into a profoundly dangerous international crisis. If the Russians take the proper action now, the British and Wall Street are dealt a tremendous defeat and the BRICS process moves a giant step forward." Beyond such potential actions by Russia, LaRouche added, "now it is time for the United States to take its historical and rightful place within a new global system of cooperation among sovereign nations for great projects financed through Hamiltonian credit. That means dumping Obama, Bush, Wall Street, and London—and getting on with a future worthy of mankind."

These words, in Russian translation, appeared Dec. 25 in the weekly newspaper *Zavtra*, under the headline, "...And Exchange Controls: Lyndon LaRouche Advises Russia What To Do." *Zavtra* noted that LaRouche had cited both Putin and Lavrov on the purpose of the sanctions being "regime change" in Russia, and had warned that this project was fraught with the danger of nuclear world war. The write-up identified LaRouche as "one of the few politicians in the West today who is publicly calling to reject the logic of confrontation and shift to one of cooperation among the main centers of the modern world—the USA, China, and Russia—for the good of all mankind."

Attention had already turned to the possibility of capital and exchange controls, at the Dec. 9 Moscow Economic Forum meeting. "Japanese Advise Putin To Make Some Arrests" and "Kotegawa: Don't Raise Rates, Jail Speculators," were headlines in Russian media coverage. The event, titled "What Is the Central Bank for Russia: Friend or Foe?", had as foreign guest speaker Daisuke Kotegawa, director of research at the Canon Institute for Global Studies and former Japanese Treasury official and IMF executive director for Japan. Academician Sergei Glazyev, an advisor to Putin, keynoted the meeting, which was attended by several State Duma committee officers; Glazyev gave a scathing follow-on to his recent article, "U.S. Sanctions and the Bank of Russia: A Double Blow Against the National Economy."

Glazyev argues that the Central Bank's declared battle against inflation is strangling the already credit-starved Russian economy. He calls for capital controls and the denomination of foreign trade in rubles, as well as earmarked Central Bank lending for productive investment—an idea repeated by Putin in his Presidential Address. According to Glazyev, "The Central Bank has a simple tool for stopping the speculation: Impose regulations on foreign-currency positions. This was done in 1998. The banks were simply forbidden to have more foreign currency in their accounts at the end of the day, than at the start."

Kotegawa, whose presentation was published in full by vestifinance.ru, contrasted the experience of Thailand during the 1997-98 currency crisis, with that of Japan. "The special guest cited an instructive story," reported agronews.ru. "In 1998, the Bank of Thailand raised its key rate to 25% and kept it there for 18 months, resulting in the destruction of the nation's industry as a whole." In Japan, however, Kotegawa reported, derivatives positions were wound up over a weekend, and speculators went to prison. In reply to a question about what the mission of the Central Bank of Japan is, Kotegawa replied, "The development of the country's industry." Commented agronews.ru, "That says it all."

International finance publications, from *Forbes* to the London *Economist*, worry aloud that Putin may yet be "inspired by Malaysia" and impose capital controls. Bloomberg on Dec. 16 quoted an op-ed by Sergei Markov, an influential think-tanker who worked in Putin's 2012 Presidential campaign, in the business newspaper *Vzglyad*: "Since the reasons for the ruble's fall are political, the response should be political, too. For example, a law that would ban Russian companies from repaying debts to Western counterparties if the ruble has dropped more than 50% in the last year. That will immediately lower the pressure on the ruble; many countries have done this. Malaysia is one example. It's in great economic shape now."

Ruslan Grinberg, the director of the Russian Academy of Science's Institute of Economics, told Channel One Russia television Dec. 17 that "standard methods won't work," but rather Russia should "revert to mandatory conversion of foreign-currency earnings to rubles; raise bank reserve requirements for engaging in forex ops; and possibly introduce licensing for permission to export foreign currency." Several members of parliament have echoed Kotegawa, calling for the investigation and jailing of speculators.

The bankrupt trans-Atlantic financiers, however, threaten to escalate. "This is only the beginning; everyone is bracing for what comes after New Year's," the *Financial Times* of London quoted an unnamed Moscow financial-sector executive on Dec. 26. In particular, the *Financial Times* projected renewed attacks on the ruble if oil prices fall again, and pointed to a the S&P rating agency's placement of Russia's sovereign debt on a watch list for possible downgrading in January.

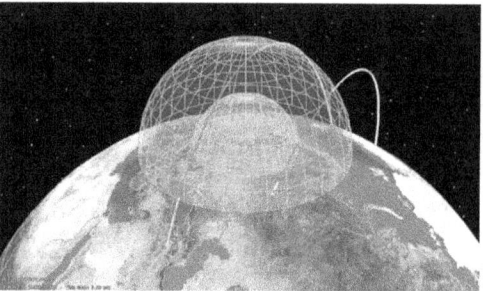

LaRouches Keynote Dubna Conference In Russia on Science, Development

by Sergei Dyshlevsky

MOSCOW, Dec. 24—Video-recorded remarks by American economist Lyndon LaRouche and a strategic presentation by Schiller Institute founder Helga Zepp-LaRouche keynoted the opening plenary session of the IV International Scientific Conference on Fundamental and Applied Problems of Sustained Development in the System Nature-Society-Man: Science, Engineering, and Education, held Dec. 22 at the Dubna International University of Nature, Society, and Man, in the Moscow Region. The annual event is organized by Professors Boris Bolshakov and Oleg Kuznetsov, associates of the late Dr. Pobisk Kuznetsov, a Russian visionary, organizer of industry, and friend of LaRouche. Both videos were greeted with applause, and several of the speakers went on to mention LaRouche as a leading thinker of our time, reflecting the widespread recognition in Russia of his record.

This year's conference was attended by over 100 scholars and students, with speakers from Belarus, Kazakhstan, and Russia. Greetings from Academician Sergei Glazyev, in his capacity as head of the Russian Academy of Sciences Scientific Council on Complex Problems of Eurasian Economic Integration, Competitiveness, and Sustained Development, were read by his colleague on the Council, Prof. Yevgeni Naumov, at the opening.

Kuznetsov, Bolshakov, Prof. Yuri Yakovets, and Prof. P.G. Nikitenko from Belarus, all touched on the current grave strategic crisis in the world. Kuznetsov, describing the world as moving along a razor's edge, said that Russia was not alone, in its economic crisis, but that such a crisis afflicts the world as a whole. He called for shifting from "the consumption society," to "a society of creating."

Yakovets, an economist, likewise described the current historical moment as "a civilizational watershed." He (rather politely) characterized the G7 countries as being "in counterphase" to the nations of Asia. Russia, he said, continues to have an am-

biguous situation: On the one hand, it has tremendous scientific potential, which has begun to be reactivated following the setbacks on the immediate post-Soviet period in the 1990s. At the same time, the speaker warned, a powerful "herd of neoliberals" persists in promoting the growth of a money-grubbing middleman layer in the economy. In his view, outside forces, disappointed in their failure so far to organize a "color revolution" in Russia, want to fan discontent by driving the Russian standard of living downwards. In this context, he charged that Russia's major banks, with their currency dealings, are operating against the national interest.

Declaring that "the age of superpowers has passed," Prof. Yakovets called for promoting scientific ties between Russia and non-Western countries, hailing efforts to establish an Academy of Science and Education of the BRICS countries (Brazil, Russia, India, China, South Africa).

'Breakthrough Technologies' Needed

Prof. Bolshakov took up the Dubna conferences' traditional theme of "sustainable development," for which the Russian term means "stable" or "sustained"

Prof. Boris Bolshakov, one of the organizers of the conference, spoke on the concept of the noösphere.

development. He drew out the difference, with its usage in the West, saying that the "Russian school of sustained development" differs from how "sustainable" development is treated in the West. "The Russian school is against the theory of 'heat death,'" said Bolshakov, adding that V.I. Vernadsky's noösphere conception should be the basis for unifying human thinking about development and overcoming the notions of a "green economy" or "zero growth."

"All countries need breakthrough technologies," Bolshakov insisted, "but for Russia, breakthrough technologies are a matter of life and death for the Russian state and Russian civilization." He called for "eliminating speculative capital." Bolshakov's proposal to replace GDP in economics by an "index of happiness" was covered in the Russian media.

There were three workshops after the plenary, one of them dedicated to the ideas of the late Pobisk Kuznetsov, the 90th anniversary of whose birth was marked earlier this year. A second session took up the legacy of the philosopher Evald Ilyenkov, likewise born in 1924, who died in 1979. In the late 1970s, the LaRouche movement's newspaper *New Solidarity*, in an article by Susan Welsh, reported on a then-revolutionary article by Ilyenkov, in the official journal *Kommunist*, about the work of Soviet psychologist Boris Meshcheryakov in educating deaf-blind children; it was startling for its departure from the precepts of materialism, delving into concept-formation in the absence of sense-certainty. A.V. Suvorov, who 40 years ago was one of the students educated by Meshcheryakov, was present at the Dubna conference and took part in this round table.

The third workshop, designed especially for young people, was on the Russian universal genius Dmitri Mendeleyev, the 180th anniversary of whose birth is this year. Its theme was planning for mankind's future, through developing new technologies.

Participants from Sevastopol, in Crimea, attending for the first time, described efforts to revitalize science on the peninsula. Other participants mentioned the ongoing crisis between Russia and Ukraine as a disaster for science, lamenting that ties with the Ukrainian scientific community have been thoroughly disrupted. Prof. Kuznetsov also emphasized that scientific ties with colleagues in the USA and Europe must not be broken, despite the current sanctions imposed against Russia.

Translated from Russian by EIR.

Lyndon LaRouche

We Have a Clear Opportunity For Greatness

Here is Lyndon LaRouche's message, videotaped Dec. 8, to the Dubna Conference, Dec. 22, 2014.

My greetings to the conference.

What we face now on a planetary scale is something completely new, something that has never happened before, we hope. Because what has happened now, we are on the brink of bringing together the major nations of the planet, the chief nations of the planet; in terms of quantity and so forth, they remain in development; but the development is remarkable, for example in South America, in elements of Africa, and some elements of Europe, especially in Russia, and some other locations, isolated locations.

But the problem is this: We have the British Empire, which is the longstanding enemy of humanity. We have to not only defeat this enemy, we also have to be able to rise to the occasion, of bringing the United States, the people of the United States, out of their present misery and disorientation, which is possible; it's feasible, it can be done. But the current government of the United States is an impossible instrument, and we've got to get rid of most of the elements which are dominating the United States government right now. We also have to emphasize that, really, what the government of the United States is, is a branch of the Saudi and British Empires, like the empires that are involved in the terror in Asia.

So therefore, what we have to think about, is the plans that we're going to make, or should be making now, which enable the world to take a fresh view of itself. The great nations which have emerged in Asia, in South America, for example, they are great nations and have great potential, but we have to protect the process. We have to eliminate the British Empire. If the British Empire's in power, there is no security. If elements of the United States, which are part of the British Empire, are there, and similar kinds of evil forces, we are in danger of losing everything, and the possibility of a thermonuclear war globally is still present.

Lyndon LaRouche: We have to enable the world to take a fresh view of itself.

Changing the Composition of the U.S. Government

Now, what I'm doing, to make it short, is I'm trying to bring about a dumping of the present United States government, because it's a rotten government and needs to be reformed. You don't need to change the design of the U.S. government; you need to change the composition of the U.S. government, especially the most recent two administrations. If that occurs, then I'm sure that the horrors faced by most of the people of the United States, and by other nations, those horrors can be defeated. The problem is, we have to defeat the enemy, the enemy which is the force we have to deal with.

I am confident we can do it. I'm confident because I know that there are capabilities in the human mind now, which are poorly understood, but are capabilities which people of some parts of the world, as in China, and some special degree, Russia, India, and so forth, and the BRICS nations—that these nations are moving in a direction of self-development, of joint self-development, which can lead to a new conception of the meaning of the human species and of our planet itself.

Things lie before us, far in this system, things lie before us which have never been dreamed by most people on this planet; but if we are fortunate, we are a few steps in scientific progress toward the greatest leap that mankind has ever defined.

For example, we know that mankind is not an animal, and no animal is mankind! We know other things about life and things and so forth, which are essential to be known. We see what's happening in China, in the development of the space exploration there: This is a revolution, which takes us in the direction of the stars. And other nations will take the same course, and follow the same course that is being done in China in this way. And that's what we have to hope for!

But it's not just hope. It's an understanding of what the great opportunities are, and the great dangers are, which lie before us.

For example, right now this woman [Victoria Nuland], who is leading and controlling part of Central Europe from the United States: an evil person. This person must be removed, must be removed from the United States and by the United States; and things like that must occur.

But my point is, I see a clear point of optimism, a clear opportunity of greatness. What we have to do, is just simply build on that, understand the actions we have to take, understand the preparations we have to make: We are on the verge of the potential of the greatest advantage in progress of mankind, which has ever been known. And we have to fight now, to make sure we secure that advantage for the sake of the future of mankind, as mankind goes out, into the higher parts of the Solar System.

Helga Zepp-LaRouche

Creating a World Worthy of the Dignity of Mankind

Helga Zepp-LaRouche gave this address, videotaped Dec. 8, to the Dec. 22, 2014 Dubna Conference.

Dear participants of the Dubna Conference,

I think you are all aware that the world is at an extremely dangerous moment, and that if the present policies of the U.S. government, the British, NATO, and the EU, were to be continued, a thermonuclear war, in all likelihood, would occur, and would lead to the extinction of civilization.

I think it is clear that both the Russian and the Chinese governments are fully aware of this danger, and if you listen to the speech President Putin gave, his annual speech to both houses of the Russian Federation, he said one thing which I think is absolutely clear: What the present crisis is all about, is not about Ukraine. He emphasized that if they would not have found the Ukraine crisis, they would have found another avenue, and that is exactly what I think is absolutely true. And I'm not saying that as an opinion, but I'm saying that as somebody who has been actively involved, together with Mr. LaRouche, for a very long time, to try to change the direction of the world towards a peace order for the 21st Century.

Now, when the Soviet Union disintegrated in 1991, we proposed an economic program which we called the Eurasian Land-Bridge, the New Silk Road, which was the idea to connect the population and industrial centers of Europe with those of Asia, through so-called "development corridors"; and in that way, we could have saved the industrial capacity of the former Comecon countries by using these capacities to build up infrastructure development corridors throughout Asia and Europe; and in that way, changed the conditions of the landlocked areas of the Eurasian continent to provide for a better living standard for all people on this continent.

Unfortunately, that was not the policy of the British and the American governments at that point, because they very clearly said, and stated, that their aim was, at that point, to turn Russia from a superpower into a raw-materials-producing Third World country. And therefore, they basically applied the first form of warfare, which was the so-called "shock therapy."

We followed that very clearly, because we had the plan to develop the Eurasian continent, and we saw that the shock therapy was never meant to do anything good to anybody, but it succeeded in reducing the Russian industrial capacities in only three years, from 1991 to 1994, to one-third of its level from '91. And what this period did, the '90s, the Yeltsin period—I think there are two very important books which describe that: One is from Sergei Glazyev,[1] and the other is from Professor

Helga Zepp-LaRouche: China has made an economic miracle which is unmatched in the world.

[Stanislav] Menshikov,[2] who was a very dear friend of ours, and who unfortunately just passed away; and they both describe that form of warfare as "genocide."

The Aim: Regime Change in Russia

The present offensive against Russia really began at the end of the '90s with the two Chechen Wars, which were financed by Boris Berezovsky, from London, and others. Also a big role was played by the American Committee for Peace in Chechnya, which was founded by the American neo-cons in 1999. Among the founding members were [Zbigniew] Brzezinski, Alexander Haig, Richard Perle, James Woolsey, Robert Kagan, who is still very important in the Obama Administration, and he is married to nobody else but Victoria Nuland. And I'm pretty sure that it is that grouping, to which President Putin referred in his recent speech, when he said that these Chechen terrorists were received on the highest level, and they were, [although] being murderers with blood on their hands, called "rebels," "freedom fighters," and so forth, by these people.

Now, the aim, already in the '90s, but especially since President Putin came back, was that of regime change in Russia, and also all the East European coun-

1. Sergei Glazyev, *Genocide: Russia and the New World Order* (EIR, 1999). Available from larouchepub.com.

2. Stansilav M. Menshikov, *The Anatomy of Russian Capitalism*, (EIR, 2006). Available from larouchepub.com.

tries where still remnants of the pro-Russian attitude existed. And the promise not to expand NATO to the borders of Russia, obviously, was broken. Victoria Nuland, the wife of Robert Kagan, who is now the Assistant Secretary of State in the State Department responsible for Europe and Eurasia, was bragging in December 2013, that the American government spent $5 billion, on Ukraine alone, for the color revolution.

The Russian military in the meantime has clearly defined color revolution as a form of war, even if it's not declared. Also, Foreign Minister [Sergei] Lavrov has clearly stated that sanctions are not a device to change the policy of Russia, but simply to topple President Putin.

Putin, in his speech, said the real aim is the Yugoslavia model for Russia, the dismemberment of the whole state; and it is also clear that the EU Association Agreement, which started and triggered the Ukraine crisis, was aimed in the same direction, because it would have flooded the Russian market with cheap European Union products, destroying important capacities in Russia.

The Ukraine crisis was entirely caused by the EU, and naturally by their American collaborators, and one can say, masters. Because the so-called Maidan was the color revolution activists, but this time, reinforced through the old Nazi networks dating back to Bandera period of the Ukrainian Nazis collaborating with the Nazi invasion in the 1940s. And these people were groomed in the entire postwar period by the CIA, by MI6, and by the BND [German foreign intelligence].

Then you had the fascist coup on the 21st February, which again was heavily controlled and sponsored by Victoria Nuland, who bragged in this famous taped phone conversation, that they wanted to put their man "Yats" [Arseniy Yatsenyuk], into office. And so, this is entirely a combined warfare-color revolution-NATO expansion to the borders of Russia, sanctions; and therefore, one should listen to the former Chief of the General Staff of the Russian Army Gen. Yuri Baluyevsky, who believes that the conflict between NATO and Russia is on the way, that it already has begun with an information war, with psychological pressure on the minds of the people, a demonization of Putin—and China, by the way—and that military force proper will be only the final stage in this process that we are already seeing today.

And when he was asked if he thinks it can be still stopped, he said, "Unfortunately, I believe it is no longer possible. The mechanism has been set in motion;

our adversaries' aims have been clearly defined: While we are alive, they will try to prevent Russia becoming their equal partner militarily or economically."

The Alternative

Fortunately, that is only one reality: It is real, but there is another one.

Since the BRICS conference, the summit in Fortaleza in Brazil this July, a whole, completely different world dynamic has been formed by the BRICS countries [Brazil, Russia, India, China, South Africa], which have now inspired many other countries in the world, the Latin American countries, the CELAC [Community of Latin American and Caribbean States], the UNASUR [Union of South American Nations], the APEC [Asia Pacific Economic Cooperation] countries (minus the United States), but also the ASEAN [Association of Southeast Asian Nations] countries, Egypt; many countries have now started to take optimism from the fact that, centered on the strategic alliance between Russia and China which was formed in May of this year, and then continued through the process of the BRICS, especially after President Xi Jinping put the offer of a New

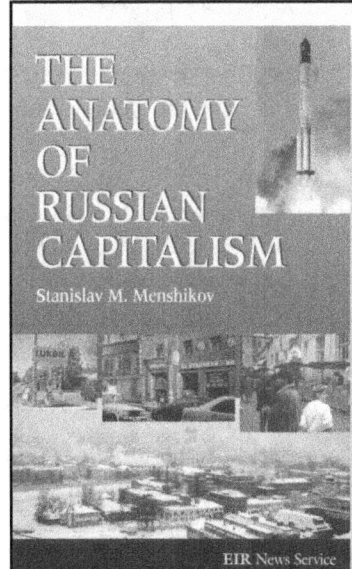

Silk Road on the table—which, by the way, is exactly what we had proposed in '91 with the Eurasian Land-Bridge/New Silk Road—a complete explosion of optimism has started among many, many countries of the developing sector.

New financial institutions are being created, or have been created already. The Asian Infrastructure Investment Bank (AIIB), the New Development Bank of the BRICS, the Shanghai Cooperation Organization bank, the New Silk Road Development Fund, the bank of the SAARC [South Asian Association for Regional Cooperation] countries—the South Asian countries; and there is right now, a complete change in the dynamic, because many projects which were intimidated by the IMF conditionalities for decades are now being realized.

China is helping to build a second Panama Canal in Nicaragua; China is helping to build a transcontinental railway from Brazil to Peru; nuclear cooperation is occurring among many, many countries. And if you look at the explosion of optimism, which, for example, is occurring in India since Narendra Modi is the Prime Minister: He has promised to build 100 new cities in India, to create 1 million jobs every month for the young people of that country; he has just announced that he will revive the 31 water-management projects which were put on ice after the assassination of Indira Gandhi.

China has accomplished an economic miracle which is unmatched in the world. China, after the Deng Xiaoping reforms, was able to transform China from a very poor country into an economic miracle, in which they accomplished in 30 years what most countries of the industrialized sector needed two centuries for. And this proposal for the New Silk Road—what China is offering is to take that Chinese economic miracle and let every country which wants to do so, participate in that effort.

After the APEC conference in Beijing, recently, Xi Jinping offered to President Obama that the United States and other major countries are all invited to participate in the New Silk Road and into these new financial mechanisms. Now, it is my firmest conviction that it is not hopeless, that that offer can be taken up.

For example, in Germany, you have right now, a complete revolt in the industry against the sanctions: Just yesterday, a new advertisement, an appeal to the government and the parliament was issued, signed by 60 important personalities from [Gerhard] Schröder, to Roman Herzog, to Horst Teltschik, the former head of the Munich Security Conference, and many others; and

the title of this appeal, by the way, is "War Again in Europe? Not in Our Name!"

So there is a resistance, and this is very important, and we have to make sure that the evil deeds of such people as Victoria Nuland are becoming known, and that we counter this war propaganda. My husband has called for the removal of Victoria Nuland, just to slow down this war machine.

Eliminate the Real Cause of War

But I think the real remedy will only come if we eliminate the real cause for this war, and that is the fact that the trans-Atlantic financial system is about to blow out. The collapse of the oil price is not only hurting Russia and Iran. It is potentially blowing out the entire trans-Atlantic financial system, because the oil companies and the shale oil producers have accumulated $1 trillion debt, which they can only pay if the oil price is between $80-120. So we are looking at a repeat of the secondary mortgage crisis of 2007.

Therefore, I believe the only real war-avoidance policy is that we get civilization into a completely new paradigm. We have to stop thinking in terms of geopolitical interests, and we have to define the common aims of mankind, and we have to define the present situation from the future: How do we want mankind to look in 10 years, in 100 years, in 1,000 years? And there, the question of joint space exploration and such things will become absolutely crucial.

Now the immediate route to go this way, is therefore to take up the offer of President Xi Jinping for the United States and Europe to join the New Silk Road. We have just produced a report which shows the unbelievable number of projects and things for the future which would change and transform the face of the Earth, and I think that this blueprint, "The New Silk Road Becomes the World Land-Bridge,"[3] is something we absolutely have to make the major issue of discussion, as the only alternative to the extinction of civilization.

I'm optimistic that we can do it. That's a guarantee I don't have, but I think it's worth the effort to try everything possible to change the agenda, and to discuss the common aims of mankind: How do we get out of this crisis, and how do we create a world which is worthy of the dignity of man, and of the identity of mankind as the only creative species in the universe.

---

3. Available from larouchepub.com

Prominent Leaders Call for U.S., Europe To Collaborate with BRICS

Dec. 26—The following release was issued on Dec. 17 by the U.S. Schiller Institute, under the title, "Prominent Leaders Back Resolution Calling for U.S. and Europe To Reject Geopolitics and Collaborate with the BRICS." As of this date, there are more than 150 prominent signers.

Dec. 17—A grouping of more than 100 prominent politicians, businessmen, academics, scientists, and artists from 20 countries have publicly endorsed a resolution calling on the U.S. and Europe to collaborate with the BRICS nations in the interest of peace and economic development. The resolution, sponsored by the Schiller Institute, was issued in response to the offer of China's President Xi Jinping for the United States to join China's New Silk Road development program, and abandon the policies of confrontation with particularly Russia and China.

The prominent signers are joined by more than 1,000 ordinary citizens from these and other nations, who urgently want their governments to abandon the policies of confrontation and collaborate with the BRICS countries, based on the Treaty of Westphalia's principle of the benefit of the other. The Schiller Institute intends to continue to garner support for the resolution from intellectual leaders and ordinary citizens alike, to create a mass movement for economic development and peace.

Helga Zepp-LaRouche, founder of the Schiller Institute, said, "The idea of collaboration with Xi Jinping's offer to cooperate with the New Silk Road is the most important peace initiative to get the world away from the edge of confrontation and war. Collaboration on this initiative is a fantastic perspective for mankind. I am calling on all people to distribute this resolution and help us get more support for it."

The list of signatures of the prominent immeidately follows.

The Petition

In today's nuclear age, the consequences of a geopolitical policy of confrontation with Russia and China can only be the thermonuclear extinction of the human race. Therefore, every effort must be made to cooperate to solve the multiple crises facing humanity.

The BRICS nations (Brazil, Russia, India, China, and South Africa) have united to pursue a policy of economic development not just for their individual countries, but for the benefit of the people of all nations. To that end, they have created a New Development Bank to invest billions in necessary development projects.

China recently initiated the Asian Infrastructure Investment Bank (AIIB), joined by over 20 Asian nations as founding members, and has set up a Silk Road Development Fund.

At the APEC [Asia-Pacific Economic] Conference in Beijing, Chinese President Xi Jinping invited President Obama to join the efforts of China and other Asian nations, including Russia, in the development of the New Silk Road.

These initiatives are not geopolitical in nature. Contrary to the Trans-Pacific Partnership (TPP) advocated by Obama, which excludes Russia and China, the BRICS-related initiatives including the Chinese proposed Free Trade Area of the Asian Pacific (FTAAP), are inclusive. They are based on the concept expressed by the late Pope Paul VI that the "new name of peace is development." Thus, in Australia at the recent G-20 meeting, both Xi Jinping and Indian Prime Minister Narendra Modi spoke of the twin goals of achieving global peace and ending poverty through economic development.

There is no problem in the world that cannot be solved by such an approach, and conversely, no problem that will be solved without it.

Such cooperation among the U.S., Russia, China, South Africa, and India, among other nations, is necessary to defeat the Ebola pandemic in Africa.

The terrorist threat represented by ISIS and al-Qaeda is aimed equally at Russia, China, and India, as well as the U.S. and Europe. It can only be defeated through a new security architecture based on cooperation.

The policy of conducting "color revolutions" under the pretext of democracy, represents a policy of war, even if that term is not used, because its aim is to topple governments with the aid of foreign money. It has to stop. The campaign to impose sanctions on Russia for its opposition to such "color revolutions," and to a Nazi coup in Ukraine, is only exacerbating the global crisis. An approach based on mutual cooperation to achieve the common ends of mankind throughout Eurasia and beyond, would instead create the basis for global peace.

While the U.S. has abandoned the Kennedy space program, the Chinese are committed to a lunar program focused on the exploitation of helium-3 for the purpose of generating unlimited fusion energy. With collaboration between the U.S., Europe, Russia, China, and India, among other nations, man could finally realize Johannes Kepler's vision of mastery of the laws of the Solar System for the benefit of man.

Only such an approach would restore the United States and Europe to their original purpose as expressed in the European Renaissance and the American Revolution, a purpose which the U.S. and Europe have increasingly abandoned, and the rest of the world has now adopted and is now urging them to re-adopt.

We therefore call upon the U.S. and Europe to abandon the suicidal geopolitical policies of the past which led to the two previous world wars, and are leading to a third, and to build a future for all humanity by re-adopting the principle of the Treaty of Westphalia, by basing foreign policy on the principle of the "benefit of the other," which ended the Thirty Years War in Europe, and on John Quincy Adams' concept of a "community of principle among sovereign nation-states."

That is the only course coherent with the true nature of man as the only creative species. Any other course is based on a concept of man as an animal, and leads to human extinction. As patriots of our own nations, and as citizens of the world, we call on our fellow citizens and the leaders of our nations to have the courage to break the current cycle of escalating bestiality, by accepting the generous offer to collaborate with the BRICS.

Prominent Signers of the Resolution

Argentina
Julio C. González, former Secretary of State; university professor, Buenos Aires
Carlos Alberto Baltazar Perez Galindo, attorney, Buenos Aires

Austria
Dr. Hans Köchler, Pres., International Progress Organization, Vienna
Michael Machura, counsellor, engineer, Österreichischer Wirtschaftsrat

Barbados
David Comissiong, Pres., Clement Payne Movement; former Senator, former Director, Commission for Pan-African Affairs

Chile
María Luz Navarrete Alarcón, V.P. of Social Security, Aquí la Gente Citizens Movement, Santiago

Colombia
Jhon Jairo Jaramillo, Prof. Liberal Arts, Univ. of el Valle

Denmark
Hugo Andersen, Director, Taarnby Karroserifabrik, Taarnby
John Scales Avery, Assoc. Prof. Emeritus, Dept. of Chemistry, Univ. of Copenhagen; chair, Danish Peace Academy
Anika Termányi Lylloff, violinist
Mohammed Mafoud, head, Danish-Syrian Union
Thomas Grønlund Nielsen, physics lecturer, Herlufsholm Skole
Jens Jorgen Nielsen, lecturer, Niels Brock Business School
Ole Skjold, former director, Ole Skjold ApS, Frederikssund
Erling Svendsen, former Pres., Danish Wheat Growers Assn., Hvalso
Ole Valentin-Hjorth, economist

France
Georges Beriachvili, pianist, Paris, Ile de France
Jacques Cheminade, Pres., Soidarité et Progrès
Col. Alain Corvez (ret.), Counsellor, international strategy and former advisor to the General-in-Command of UNIFIL
Pierre Eboundit, Pres., Pan-African League, Umoja, Reims
Ali Rastbeen, Pres., Geopolitical Academy of Paris
Dr. Louis Reymondon, honorary surgeon of French hospitals; Pres., VietAmitié (France-Vietnam Friendship Assn.)
Jean-Jacques Seymour, radio journalist, Paris
Bassam Tahhan, Franco-Syrian Prof. of Geostrategy, Ecole nationale supérieure des techniques avancées (ENSTA), Paris

Germany
Wolfgang Effenberger, publicist, Bavaria
Dr. Josef Gruber, Prof. Emeritus, Hagen

Ekaterina Medvedeva-Schwerbock, actress, Berlin

Alena Petrova, General Director, Art Assemblee Agency, GmbH, Baden-Württemberg

Dorothea Schleifenbaumm, County Councilwoman, Siegen-Wittgenstein

Dr. Gallus Strobel, Mayor, Triberg, Baden-Wurtemberg

Dmitris Tzamouranis, Greek visual artist, Berlin

H.C. von Sponeck, former UN Assistant Secretary General

Prof. Dr. Carl-Otto Weiss, Research Director, Physikalisch-Technische Bundesanstalt (PTB), Braunschweig

Helga Zepp-LaRouche, founder, Schiller Inst., Wiesbaden

Greece
Leonidas Chrysanthopoulos, Ambassador (ret.); Political Secretariat of EPAM (United People's Front)

Panos Kammenos, Pres., Independent Greeks; Member, Hellenic Parliament, Athens

Lefteris Karayannis, Ambassador (ret.); diplomatic advisor to Panos Kammenos, Athens

Theodore Katsanevas, chair, Drachma Five Star, Athens

Gen. Konstantinos Konstantinides (ret.), Generals Against Nuclear War

Dr. George Pararas-Carayannis, chair, 6th International Tsunami Symposium; Pres., Tsunami Society International; editor, *Science of Tsunami Hazards*

Dr. George Tsobanoglou, V.P., International Sociological Assn., Research Committee on Sociotechnics/ Sociological Practice

Guinea
Jacques Bacamurwanko, former Ambassador of Burundi to the U.S., N.Y.

India
Dr. Vinod Saighal, Exec. Dir., Eco Monitors Society, New Delhi

Arun Shrivastava, author, New Delhi

Ireland
Eugene Douglas, LaRouche Irish Brigade, Armagh

Italy
Antonella Banaudi, opera singer, Sanremo

Gabriele Chiurli, Tuscany Regional Council, Arezzo

Nino Galloni, economist, Rome

Alfonso Gianni, Director, Cercare Ancora Foundation, Rome

Tiberio Graziani, Pres., Inst. of Advanced Studies in Geopolitics, Rome

Enzo Siviero, National Council of Universities, Padua

Valentina Iorio Tomasetti, City Councilwoman, Galliate Lombardo

Malaysia
Chandra Muzaffar, Pres., International Movement for a Just World, Kuala Lumpur

Mexico
Luis Benito Acosta Jiménez, agronomist, Director General, Agronomy Federation of Mexico City

Carlos Arellano Palma, architectural engineer, Mexican Assn. of Engineers, Mexico City

Esteban Palma Bautista, civil engineer, Mexican Assn. of Engineers, Mexico City

Gaston Pardo-Pérez, journalist, *Reseau Voltaire*, Veracruz, Coatepec

Rosa Elia Romero Guzmán, Federal Congresswoman, Oaxaca

Netherlands
Yufang Guo, chair, Jomec International, Rotterdam

Nicaragua
José Francisco Rosales Argüello, V.P., COPPPAL; Justice, Nicaragua Supreme Court

Panama
Mario Rognoni, journalist, businessman, engineer, Panama City

Paraguay
Julio A. Mendoza, architect, Pres., Chamber of Housing and Infrastructure of Paraguay

Russia
Sergei Cherkasov, Deputy Director for Research, State Geological Museum, Russian Academy of Sciences, Moscow

Guzel A. Danukalova, Inst. of Geology, Ufa Scientific Center, Russian Academy of Sciences, Ufa

Victor Kuzin, head, Moscow Bureau for the Defense of Human Rights without Borders, Moscow

Stanislav N. Nekrasov, Prof.; Chair, International Legal and Futurological Information Agency, Yekaterinburg

Alexander D. Petrushin, Inst. for Demography, Migration, and Regional Development, Moscow

Sergey Pulinets, Space Research Inst., Russian Academy of Sciences, Moscow

Sergei V. Zaitsev, Inst. of Solid State Physics, Russian Academy of Sciences, Chernogolovka, Moscow Region

Olga Zinovieva, co-chair, Rossiya Segodnya Zinoviev Club, Moscow

Slovak Republic
Jan Carnogursky, former Czechoslovak dissident; former Slovak Justice Minister

Spain
Sebastian Martin, Director, Noticanarias.com, Puerto del Rosario, Islas Canarias

Javier Otazu Ojer, Economics Prof., UNED, Pamplona

Fructuoso Rodríguez Morales, former leader, Transport Union (ret.), Las Canarias

Sweden
Greger Ahlberg, architect, Stockholm

Leena Malkki-Guignard, producer, opera singer, Operafabriken, Malmo

Ukraine
Vladimir R. Marchenko, Confederation of Labor of Ukraine, Kiev

Natalia M. Vitrenko, Doctor of Economics; Chairman, Progressive Socialist Party of Ukraine, Kiev

United States
Morad Abou-Sabe, Arab American League of Voters of N.J.

Amer Aboud, Syrian American Forum Chicago, Ill.

Fidel Acevedo, Co-Chair, Progressive Hispanic Caucus, Texas Democratic Party

Ramatu Ahmed, Founder, Federation of African Muslim Women in America, New York, N.Y.

Nathaniel Batchelder, Director, Oklahoma City Peace House, Oklahoma City, Okla.

Roseanne Barr, comedian, former Presidential candidate, Peace and Freedom Party, Hawaii

Robert Beltran, actor, director, Los Angeles, Calif.

George Bioletto, trustee, International Assn. of Machinists, Long Beach, Calif.

Kofi A. Boateng, PhD, African Federation, Inc., Ossining, N.Y.

Elena Branson, Pres., Russia Center, New York, N.Y.

Howard Chang, Prof. of Hydraulic Engineering (ret.), San Diego State Univ., Calif.

Victor Chang, Prof. Univ. of Southern Calif. (ret.), Director, Inst. of Sino Strategic Studies, Los Angeles, Calif.

Ramsey Clark, US Attorney General, 1967-69, New York, N.Y.

Jaime Contreras, Bus. Rep., Painters Union, Las Vegas; Chapter Coordinator, Labor Council for Latin American Advancement, Las Vegas, Nev.

Hal Cooper, transportation engineer, Advisory Board, Freight Transportation Division, Seattle, Wash.

Brian Crowell, teacher, former Shop Steward, AFT Local 1078, Berkeley, Calif.

Dr. Fred Dallmayr, Co-Chair, World Public Forum, Dialogue of Civilizations, South Bend, Ind.

Dr. Bill Deagle, Genesis Communication Network, host, Nutri-Medical Report, Calif.

T. Herbert Dimmock, Founder, Music Director, Bach Concert Series, Baltimore, Md.

E. Leopold Edwards, faculty (ret.), Howard Univ., Washington, D.C.

James H. Fetzer, PhD, McKnight Prof. Emeritus, Univ. of Minnesota, Duluth

James Fox, Pres., American Fertilizer Trade, LLC, Great Neck, N.Y.

Cornelius Gallagher, Member of Congress, 1959-73, N.J.

Habib Ghanim, Sr., Pres., D.C. Halal Chamber of Commerce, Silver Spring, Md.

Donald Gibson, Prof. Emeritus, Univ. of Pittsburgh; author, *Wealth, Power, and the Crisis of Laissez Faire Capitalism*, et al., Greensburg, Pa,

Nitin Gujaran, Pres., Assn. for India's Development, MIT, Cambridge, Mass.

George C. Hillman, MBA, entrepreneur, Boston, Mass.

Jim Hogue, host, WGDR radio Plainfield, Vt.

Lok Home, Pres., Robbins Co., Solon, Ohio

Hunter Huang, Pres., National Assn. for China's Peaceful Unification, Washington, D.C.

Fred Huenefeld, member, State Democratic Party Central Committee, Monroe, La.

Rep. Thomas Jackson, State Rep., Ala.

Constance Johnson, State Senator (ret.), District 48, Okla.

Ralph Johnson, engineer, nuclear industry, Seattle, Wash.

Sam Kahl, District Leader, Democratic Party of Multnomah County, Portland, Ore.

Sang Joo Kim, Founder, Director, Inst. for Corean-American Studies

Fred Kaviani, sales manager, Surface Transportation Systems, Monogram Systems, Los Angeles, Calif.

George Krasnow, Pres., Russian-American Goodwill Assn.

Keerthana Krishnan, Executive Director, Assn. for India's Development, MIT, Cambridge, Mass.

Lyndon H. LaRouche, Jr., economist, statesman, Round Hill, Va.

Eric Larsen, author, *The Skull of Yorick: The Emptiness of American Thinking at a Time of Grave Peril*, New York, N.Y.

LeMar Lemmons III, at-large member, former Pres., Detroit Board of Public Education; former member, Michigan House of Representatives, Detroit

Ed Lozansky, PhD, Pres. and founder, American Univ., Moscow; founder, World Russia Forum, Washington, D.C.

Wayne Madsen, publisher and editor, *The Wayne Madsen Report*

Clyde Magarelli, former Director of War Studies, William Paterson Univ.; author, Prof. of Sociology, Wayne, N.J.

Mike Manypenny, member, West Virginia House of Delegates

Vance McAllister, former U.S. Rep. (2013-14), Monroe, La.

Thomas Grolund Miner, chairman, CEO, Thomas H. Miner Assn., Inc., Chicago, Ill.

Saket Mishra, Assn. for India's Development, MIT, Cambridge, Mass.

Anthony Morss, Music Director, Principal Conductor, N.J.; Assn. of Verismo Opera, Inc., New York, N.Y.

Theo Mitchell, Esq., former State Senator, Greenville, S.C.

Jeff Monroe, State Senator, S.D.

Somnath Mukherji, Assn. for India's Development, MIT, Cambridge, Mass.

Robert Newton, former V.P., CWA, Local 2252, Oakton, Va.

Nomi Prins, author, *All the Presidents' Bankers: The Hidden Alliances that Drive American Power*

Earl D. Rasmussen, P.E., Exec. V.P. Eurasia Center, Lt. Col. (ret.), U.S. Army, Falls Church, Va.

Ganga P. Ramdas, PhD,, Prof. of Economics, Lincoln Univ., Philadelphia, Pa.

Philip Restino, VFP 136, co-chair, Vets for Peace, Daytona, Fla.

Kesha Rogers, former candidate for Democratic nomination to U.S. Senate, Houston, Tex.

Natalie Sabelnik, Russian-American community leader, San Francisco, Calif.

Ranjani Saigal, Exec. Dir., Ekal Vidyalaya Foundation of the USA, Burlington, Mass.

Jose I. Sangerman, PhD, biologics researcher, Boston, Mass.

Keith L. Shaffer, former Pres., IAM local 1784, Baltimore, Md.

Prashant Shah, publisher, *India Tribune*, Chicago, Ill.

Vaithilingam Shanmuganathan, National Committee member, Liberal Party of Sri Lanka; Secretary General, Liberal Democratic Workers Union of Sri Lanka; former Advisor to the Governor of the Central Bank of Sri Lanka, Azusa, Calif.

Randy Sowers, owner, South Mountain Creamery, Middletown, Md.

Baifeng Sun, Director, The Confucius Inst., U. Mass. Boston

Rosemarie Swanger, Pennsylvania State Rep. (ret.)

Dr. John Telford, Superintendent (ret.) Detroit Public Schools, Mich.

Judith Van Dyke Assn. of Small Entrepreneurs, Syracuse, N.Y.

Bob Van Hee, Alderman, former City Council Pres., Redwood Falls, Minn.

Anil Verma, Pres., Anil Verma Associates, Inc., Los Angeles, Calif.

Pat Wadsworth, Secretary, Grays Harbor Democrats, Wash. State

Joanne Wilder, Editor, *The Patriot*, N.Y.

Wang Chung Ping, Pres., Inst. Sino Strategic Studies, Los Angeles, Calif.

Lynn J. Yen, Executive Director, Foundation for the Revival of Classical Culture, New York, N.Y.

Lowell Young, Treasurer, Mariposa County Democratic Central Committee, Calif.

Venezuela

Román Rojas Cabot, former Ambassador to the European Union, and to Guyana, Caracas

EIREconomics

Oil Prices, Derivatives Light Fuse on Wall Street Time Bomb

by Paul Gallagher

Dec. 30—It is becoming clear to more experts on debt in the trans-Atlantic banking system, that the outrageous mid-December power play by which Wall Street banks forced Congress to grant FDIC insurance to their commodity and credit derivatives, was directly linked to the oil and gas price collapse. This outrage in Congress may lead to the government bailing out Wall Street banks in crisis, sooner than any of the suborned members of Congress thought when they went along with urgent telephone calls from JPMorgan Chase CEO Jamie Dimon and from the Obama White House. The impact of the oil price collapse in the derivatives markets is a time-bomb for an already bankrupt Wall Street.

That mid-December bribery-and-corruption orgy was led by Citigroup, JPMorgan Chase, and Morgan Stanley banks (along with their stickman, Barack Obama). Those three banks, along with Goldman Sachs, are the most exposed to oil/gas sector debt—which has been ballooning by an average $100 billion in net new debt per year for a decade—and to $20 trillion in risky commodity derivatives exposure which has now put them in trouble. Citibank has the largest oil debt exposure, approximately 7% of its total asset book, and Citi was at the center of the "budget bill" wing-ding which put the Federal government back on the hook for the coming commodity derivatives losses by these banks. Citigroup is now the target of a "break up Citigroup" campaign proposed by MIT economist Simon Johnson and which will have some bipartisan support in the Senate of the new Congress.

The oil price collapse began in late October as the collusion by U.S. officials with Saudi Arabia's monarchy to hit Russia with an "oil sanction"; but it has gone out of their control. Notably, on Dec. 20, it was not Russia whose credit was downgraded, but the European oil majors BP, Total, and Shell, all placed on negative credit watch by Standard and Poor's. The oil majors have been loading up with debt for a decade, with an emphasis on paying dividends and buying back their own stock. That debt was piled up despite the fact that demand for oil and gas, throughout the trans-Atlantic economies, has become more and more depressed since the 2007-08 financial collapse. The sector now has roughly $1.6 trillion in debt with—*if oil prices remain in the $50 per barrel range*—not much more than $300 billion in revenues, a highly leveraged situation. Keep in mind that during December, the natural gas price has also plunged by a third, down to the range of $3/cubic foot.

Junk Debt Markets Shake

The "front end" of this debt bubble problem is in the North American shale sector, whose production of oil and gas is less efficient, more expensive, and more environmentally damaging than the industry as a whole. Here bankruptcies of drilling and rig companies are already occurring and the debt in trouble is highly leveraged and high-interest (junk bonds and leveraged loans). It is, along with long-term, high-interest auto loans, essentially the banks' subprime debt bubble of this decade. These two subprime sectors have been dominating new capital investment and employment creation in the U.S. economy. The *Wall Street Journal* on Dec. 17, in "Junk Bond Worries Spread Beyond Oil," reported that these sectors of debt, totalling about $2.4 trillion, have actually started to contract, after rising sharply from 2011 through mid-2014.

London *Telegraph* financial analyst Andrew Critchlow warned already on Nov. 14 that oil shale drillers had come to be nearly one-third of all "high-yield, sub-investment grade" (subprime) borrowers in the United States. He estimated that if the oil price stayed in the $60s (it has been in the $50s for more than a month), 30% of high-yield B- and CCC-grade (energy) borrowers would default. "A shock of that magnitude could be sufficient to trigger a broader high-yield market default cycle," Critchlow warned.

That the Wall Street banks are being hit by this, was shown by the end-of-November report—ironically, put out by Citibank's research team—that the U.S. banking sector's revenue had dropped by 17% in the third quarter, and its loan revenue, the area which has been dominated by high-interest lending to the energy sector, had dropped by 60%. At the same time, the banking sector's exposure to foreign exchange derivatives rose by 90%, and to commodity derivatives by 40%.

This highly dangerous situation for the banks goes back to the Federal Reserve's allowing the big Wall Street banks to own commodities and commodities infrastructure (warehouses, tankers, electric utility plants, etc.), by giving them waivers of the Bank Holding Company Act in the 2002-05 period.

This ownership of commodities by banks—which are also controlling the debt, futures, and derivatives markets for the same commodities at the same time—was the subject of highly condemnatory hearings in Sen. Carl Levin's (D-Mich.) Permanent Investigations Subcommittee in the waning days of the 113th Congress.

These Wall Street practices, which the Glass-Steagall Act also prohibited to commercial banks, allowed the big banks to run up key commodity prices and, at the same time, collect large secondary profits (from derivatives markets) on the commodity prices they were manipulating.

They also put the banks in danger of being hit by huge losses in case of certain "commodity catastrophes," like the breakup of a large oil tanker with a massive oil leak, for example.

Wearing Heavy 'Collars'

But a very large price shock for which the banks' trading programs are not prepared, is the biggest danger to them.

In 2012 the Federal Reserve began publicly "debating" the possibility of forcing the banks out of commodities and infrastructure holdings, but did nothing about it. The Fed "advised" the Wall Street banks to get out of commodity holdings; the banks ignored this. While JPMorgan Chase exited some commodity holdings which had just cost it large fines for market manipulation, Goldman, Citi, and Morgan Stanley went deeper into commodity holdings.

In 2013, the Fed started jawboning Wall Street to stop making massive amounts of "leveraged loans," which were going most heavily to energy firms related to the "shale boom" or to similarly inefficient wind power and solar power schemes. The Fed has admitted publicly that the banks ignored this "advice" as well.

With the collapse of the oil price by 50% in the second half of 2014, the banks have found that a widespread type of commodity derivative known as a "three-way collar" has become very dangerous to them. As the price has declined, from $110/barrel for West Texas Intermediate Crude all the way down to below $55/barrel now, these derivatives have compelled the banks not only to buy more leveraged debt paper, but to buy more oil and gas futures as well.

According to financial experts, the immediate prospect of losses from defaulting debt in the leverage loan and junk bond markets, together with the only slightly longer-term prospect of huge losses in the derivatives markets, have put the Wall Street banks in trouble. The latter's losses could be in the hundreds of billions in total, given that this derivatives exposure of Wall Street is in the trillions.

The biggest U.S. banks, which now reportedly have some $240 trillion in derivatives exposure, have been allowed to pile up almost all of it on their FDIC-insured commercial banking units since Glass-Steagall was eliminated in the 1990s. But due to their extreme risk, these *commodity* derivatives were among the few types that could not be in those depository units—until the banks ran roughshod over Congress in mid-December. Now, with potentially huge losses looming, those trillions in derivatives are subject to a crisis Federal bailout.

Food Prize Laureate: Prerequisites For Solving the World Food Crisis

Dr. Sanjaya Rajaram, eminent plant scientist, was awarded the World Food Prize in October 2014, in Des Moines, Iowa, for "for his scientific research that led to a prodigious increase in world wheat production, by more than 200 million tons, building upon the successes of the Green Revolution." The prize was established in 1986 by Dr. Norman E. Borlaug (1914-2009), father of the Green Revolution. Dr. Rajaram, born in India, came in 1969 to work in Mexico with Dr. Borlaug, and became a citizen there.

Following the announcement in Summer 2014, that Dr. Rajaram would be the 2014 World Food Prize Laureate, he gave an interview on Aug. 8, 2014 at his offices in the state of Mexico, to Fabiola Ramirez and Carolina Dominguez, for the magazine "IO, Estadismo, Ciencia y Arte" ("IO, Statecraft, Science and Art" of the LaRouche Citizens Movement of Mexico (MOCILA), which made it available to EIR.

Q: First, we would like to ask you about the World Food Prize, also known as the Nobel Prize of Agriculture, which will be awarded to you Oct. 16 in Iowa. Can you talk to us about the research that won you this award?

Rajaram: I am truly very happy with the recognition, but I want to add—and make very clear—that the award is not just for my work. I was the lead man, but other scientists have to be recognized, especially the International Maize and Wheat Improvement Center

Dr. Sanjaya Rajaram speaking Oct. 16, 2014, at the ceremony in Des Moines, Iowa, at which he received the World Food Prize.

(CIMMYT), and another international agency on drought which is in Nicaragua, and also many other countries that collaborated. And principally, the farmers from the Yaqui Valley, from the Mexicali and Bajío valleys, with whom I have worked; and those from Punjab, India, and from other places. I will be accepting the award in all of their names.

Why did the committee recognize this achievement? After the Green Revolution, during the period in which I led research into wheat and its development, the world was able to produce 200 million more tons of wheat. That is a great advance in the availability of world food. Many countries, more than 50 of them, benefitted from this development, including Mexico.

The Borlaug Tradition

Q: With U.S. President Franklin D. Roosevelt's Good Neighbor Policy, under the leadership of then-Vice President Henry Wallace, who had a broad knowledge of agriculture and technological improvements in the field, a process of international scientific collaboration among various nations was launched, such as the Inter-American Center for Agricultural Cooperation in Costa Rica. And of course, in Mexico, there was the CIMMYT, under the leadership of Dr. Norman Borlaug, a great scientist, visionary, and humanist, also known as the Father of the Green Revolution, through which millions of people facing starvation were able to be saved. As someone who carries on the tradition of

FIGURE 1
Wheat Yields in Developing Countries, 1950-2004

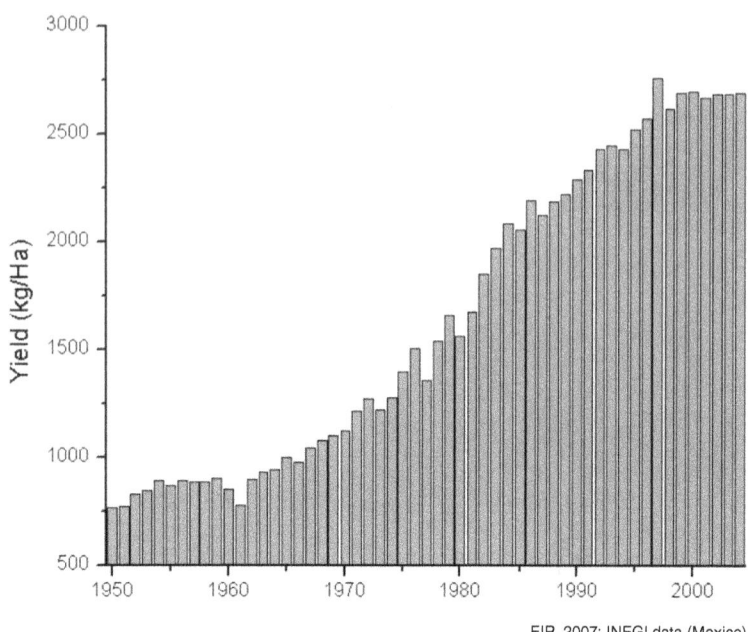

EIR, 2007; INEGI data (Mexico)

this humanist current, will you tell us about your work and friendship with Dr. Borlaug?

Rajaram: When I first arrived in Mexico in 1969, I was a youth of 27 years, recently graduated from the University of Sydney in Australia. Dr. Borlaug did not interview me, but he had heard of me through Prof. Irving Armstrong Watson, who was a professor at Sydney University, under whom I received my doctoral degree. They knew each other, and that is how he heard of me, and that's why Borlaug was interested in bringing me here, to Mexico, under a two-year post-doctorate program.

I began to work with him, knowing no Spanish, from a family which knew nothing of Mexican customs. I had to first learn the language, something my family made a priority; that was the basis upon which I became very interested in Mexican culture.

Then, at the beginning, working with Norman Borlaug, my idea was that I was just training myself to learn all I could from him of his knowledge and philosophy, because although he wasn't a Nobel winner in 1960—he received this honor a year later—I nonetheless recognized that he was the best there was in the genetic improvement of wheat. And so learning everything there was to learn from him became a challenge, and then I would have to leave in just a few years.

And yet, look, I am still here! Because in 1973—actually just five kilometers south of here where the CIMMYT is based—Norman and his assistant director, Dr. Glenn Anderson, called me in one day, and said, "Raja"—not Rajaram, which was too difficult for him—"I want you to head up the wheat flour program." Naturally, I was very surprised, as I wasn't trained, so we struck a deal to work together in the beginning. I told him, "Look Dr. Borlaug, I don't have sufficient training to handle an international program in corn and wheat improvement. You've won a Nobel Prize. Who am I to do this? But if you promise to help me for two or three years, I will have a sense of how to lead this program." And so I began.

I have tremendous respect for Dr. Borlaug, since he taught me everything he knew. I had a good knowledge of plant genetics, phytopathology, and other sciences, but learning with him in the field was a success. We worked five kilometers outside of Toluca or in the Yaqui Valley, working from 6:00 in the morning until 6:00 in the evening, because that was what he was like; and in fact, he had chosen me because I could match him in the field. He not only saw my ability, but also my tenacity; someone who could do the work well.

And so we began. This collaboration lasted until 2007. Although Dr. Borlaug retired, he stayed, in one form or another. He didn't tell me what to do and I didn't have to do what he said, but we did discuss everything, especially at the Mr. Steak restaurant in Ciudad Obregón, over steak and tequila. I can tell you that these were good times, discussing agricultural questions.

Q: I saw a report about a visit you made to Obregón to talk about Borlaug's centennial (2014), and you said there, that though he was retired, he continued to follow how the work was going.

Rajaram: He assured me that he would come, because he was very wise. He read many things. (He didn't have much time to read at that time. We couldn't do everything, because we spent a lot of time in the field. But when he retired, he began to read a lot.)

I was fascinated to learn about his philosophy of how to integrate, among different disciplines, the sciences of agriculture, anthropology, archaeology, geo-

Dr. Norman Borlaug (right) in the field with Dr. Sanjaya Rajaram, his successor as head of CIMMYT's wheat program. They studied data at the Ciudad Obregón experiment station in the 1990s.

graphical history, weather; and I became very interested in nutrition, fertilizer, water. Norman was top notch, and knew how to put it all together.

I don't take this [award] as a follow-on or continuation of the Green Revolution. That would not have been a great success, and the World Food Prize is not to recognize the status quo; there had to be an advance. And that advancement, was not just by me as a scientist. I relied on an international organization, on national programs, advanced countries, and the farmers; together, we were able to achieve it.

We never forgot that scientists don't produce food, but farmers do, and we have to learn what they are thinking and how we are able to help them. Norman always talked with the farmers; I learned from him that the farmer is number one. I began to work in the Yaqui Valley, first with the youth, and afterwards the elders also accepted me.

Q: What kind of collaboration have you had with other scientists and international organizations, and with governments, first, when you were with the CIMMYT, and now, when you are in the private sector and your company is dedicated to researching and developing products that are tested in the field?

Rajaram: I learned at the CIMMYT, and also in what then was in Syria, but now is in Amman, Jordan, and in Lebanon and Morocco, due to the war occurring there. I learned that we have to deal with agriculture through institutions; at times one can work with the farmers, but without national institutions, where do the farmers go?

For example, when I began my scientific work and my leadership in the Yaqui Valley, I knew that I had to work with the INIFAP [National Institute for Innovation in Forestry, Agriculture, and Livestock], which is a government office there. I thought that they should work with the farmers. I approached the farmers and told them it was very important to work with the institutions. My main success when I worked with CIMMYT is that I globalized the wheat work in the CIMMYT. Now I work for a private company, but we never forget that whether from the public or the private sector, we all have to help the farmers. They have to buy seed; no one gives it to them as a present.

Through Resource Seeds, I have agreements with private-sector institutions, but since I came out of the public sector, out of CIMMYT, I also sometimes give my products to people who want to work with them. Sometimes I give them to CIMMYT so that they can use them in their hybrids. I work with the private sector in India, Australia, California, Mexicali, Ciudad Obregón. I wanted to complement current technology in the Yaqui Valley, not replace it; to complement what the government and the CIMMYT were doing. I saw that we could create something which could complement that.

Look Ahead, Prepare the Youth

Q: Norman Borlaug once said that we believed that we had discovered everything about biotechnology until what he called the "monster UG99" appeared in Uganda. Surely there are other diseases that we don't know about yet. The concern is that we are not preparing the next generation of youth in the relevant areas, encouraging creativity so that they can make the discoveries of new technologies that will defend humanity from those monsters that want to eat our food. So, for the coming generations, what do you think about the research into nuclear mutations, and your opinion about NASA and space science with regard to research into cultivation on board space stations? And what do you consider the priority for research as a challenge to youth?

Rajaram: You have a whole mix of questions there. Norman was convinced, and I am as well, that if we do not correctly prepare the youth, if we do not inject new ideas and inventions, we are not going to move forward. The question would be: Do we have sufficient, good educational institutions to be able to train new generations of researchers, so that they can confront new problems?

For example, we all know that there are climate problems, which are going to change. Some don't accept that; I do. Climate change is going to be very drastic. Perhaps the temperature average will stay the same, but even a slight rise or decline of 2-3° might, perhaps, destroy crops through frost. This kind of problem requires a different scientific focus. This is one example; it could be something else. It could be a lack of nutrients in the soil; our soil is already depleted. We need well-trained agronomists to do good work.

Therefore, train youth in the reality that the climate is going to change. There are more people, nutrition has to increase—things like that.

So, we have to make sure that our youth are coming out of the universities well trained, and if they are not, what are we going to do? You can answer this question. I see that there are many institutions, but few are prepared to achieve this. We are not talking about the number of scientists that are graduating, the youth that graduate; we need quality. We have to say this, without naming anybody.

Now, speaking of biotechnology, as I said, there have been many inventions in the past 100, 200 years, but there is always resistance on the part of people to new things. Remember that they wanted to send Galileo to jail, or to execute him. So the attacks on biotechnology today do not surprise me.

I say that we can base our policy on science, on knowledge, good knowledge which protects our nutrition, our environment, everything. And at the same time, if production is being increased, if we want this kind of science to be applied, we can't reject it. We have to study it well, to prepare ourselves. Not me anymore, but young people have to know what's what and what must be done.

What I can say, is that today, we have to manage our resources and train people well, so that they will work with the farmers—not just working on crops but also with the farmers—because, as I said, they are the ones who produce the food. They are the ones who take care of the soil; they are the ones who have to apply the water; they have animals in their homes and surroundings.

And we also have to take care of all the resources that are on our planet, and all the things in the sea. I don't know how to fish. I've never caught a fish, but I like fish. We must take care of our resources.

I'm convinced that the planet can support more people, as long as we manage our resources well; we can implement good policies, in economics, as you talk about, and in our universities, and have good educational systems so that we are up to standard.

Yes, that's what we have to do, and we have to do it soon, if we—all countries—are not to lose the battle.

Food Sovereignty

Q: I want to address the question of state intervention—the participation of sovereign states with respect to the food crisis—in order to achieve food self-sufficiency.

The World Trade Organization met in Geneva, Switzerland, on July 26, where India decided not to sign the WTO's trade protocol, which asserts there are to be no subsidies for farmers, nor for food stocks for the poor of that nation.

The WTO asserts this genocidal policy in the name of free trade. The WTO doesn't speak about food self-sufficiency, but about food "security," by which they mean only "market access."

In this regard, I read an interview with Dr. Robert Zeigler of the International Rice Research Institute (IRRI) in the Philippines, where he spoke about the crisis of 2007 as regards access to markets, which didn't work. He said, "In 2007, Vietnam did not produce what it was going to, they stopped exporting; a hurricane or a weather event hit Bangladesh. India knew that it was going to need food, and they were not going to export. The Philippines requested millions of tons, and that caused an international panic." Zeigler made the point that, even if people have money to buy food, what if there is no food to be found?

Would you comment on this distinction between food self-sufficiency and food security, which is not at all a subtle difference?

Rajaram: Look, we need both. We need food security within nations, utilizing all possible resources. We can't have a policy that goes against this, because oth-

A farmer in Mexico in 2010, tilling his field with an off-set disc.

Creative Commons/CIMMYT, Fonseca

who leave have to be trained in other areas, to provide other services, perhaps working in a hotel, building a highway, maybe constructing a dam, or anything else. They have to have opportunities.

So, we can talk about when there is food, or when we have to import food. We can talk about that, because we are not going to *give it*, they are going to *buy it*. And here is Norman's great criticism of the Indian government: They thought of producing such an amount [self-sufficiency in 1974], and that then the world would be fine. And that was pure "blah, blah, blah," since millions of people are dying for lack of jobs; that has to be thought about. Every country has to think about jobs, Mexico included.

Q: During the 1980s, Mexico achieved food self-sufficiency under President [José] López Portillo's Mexican Food System (SAM), which increased production. By the end of that government, we had achieved unprecedented economic growth, and President López Portillo issued an international call, during a speech at the United Nations, asking for the creation of a new, and more just, financial system that would allow nations to grow in all basic areas. What do you think of that period of food self-sufficiency under SAM? Could this be revived to begin a new policy of food self-sufficiency today?

Rajaram: It is very difficult for me to answer that question. Look, whatever policy is taken and whatever government decision is made that allows us to efficiently produce food, and also for the farmers to live better, I'm all for that policy. Sometimes there are changes, sometimes a policy could be very good, but it has implications.

I am not criticizing President López Portillo's policy. Actually, I am not very well informed about the period you are now telling me about; but I would like to see the best technology, and better inputs for the farmers, be available when needed; training for the farmers to know how to do their work better; that the policy be that of providing prices which enable farmers to move forward, too.

The farmer can't just have losses; he has to educate

erwise, we end up with a lot of unemployed people. For example, a change in policy is possible in our country, but at the same time, to some degree we do have regulation of free trade so that food can be moved around when needed, in order not to depend completely on foreign sources. Where is the separation between the two? There has to be a combination, because, as I said, climate change is going to be devastating.

There are problems, even if a country is able to export its surplus. Let's take the example of Australia, which exports between 12 and 20 million tons of wheat a year. However, a drought could dramatically reduce this. Then a controlled chain reaction begins. For another example, the decline in production in Russia several years ago led to a wheat shortage worldwide. It is very important to know all this, to be able to deploy. Naturally, a country that produces more has to sell at a price that is fair for its farmers, without blackmailing them.

I do agree that merely having sufficient grain in a country does not necessarily guarantee that the whole world is going to have food. To achieve this, we need jobs, and we also need to train youth so that they can take better jobs, because some youth don't know how to do anything, and then what are they going to do? Grow crops with a stick? It can't stay that way forever. From my viewpoint, we have to mechanize agriculture if we want to be efficient, and this means we are not going to have a lot of people in the countryside, so those people

his children. When we talk about food, we can't just talk about having three meals a day. We need clothing, we should have a house, we must send our children to school, give them opportunities. We won't be able to move part of our population into other kinds of services or jobs if we don't do this.

If we don't do this, there will always be division in the country; we don't want this. There must be a policy so that if the population is leaving the countryside to work in other areas, to have other kinds of work, so that the quantity of our arable land remains the same or is greater. I want any government, current or future, to do its best for Mexico.

Immoral Attacks on the Green Revolution

Q: The organization called GLOBE (Global Legislators Organization for a Balanced Environment), is a group of legislators founded on the initiative of former U.S. Vice President Al Gore. In its document called "Natural Capital of Mexico," it attacks the Green Revolution, saying: "The results of the Green Revolution enabled production to increase notably, although it had no impact on the poorest of the poor; whereas its environmental consequences were very harmful because of the contamination of soil and of water produced by the abuse of agrochemicals and, moreover, they are inefficient energy systems." How would you respond to this?

Rajaram: It is very easy, perhaps, for an organization whose people probably live in an ivory tower, to say that this was bad, that it hurt the poor. This isn't true.

Take the example of India, whose wheat production has increased almost nine times since 1965, when it began its Green Revolution, which was transplanted Mexican technology. This involved not just seeds, but also the use of water and fertilizer, which enabled this

Dr. Norman E. Borlaug, giving the keynote address at the Ministerial Conference and Expo on Agricultural Science and Technology, June 2003. He said, "The world has the technology, either available or well-advanced in the research pipeline, to feed 10 billion people. Extending the Green Revolution to the Gene Revolution will provide a better diet at lower prices to many more food-insecure people." He received the Nobel Peace Prize in 1970 for his wheat improvements.

growth to happen.

So, tell me: Today, if we had not implemented an advanced technology, or if we do not continue it in the future, who will be the first to want to die? Because this planet isn't producing enough for everybody. Someone has to say, "Look, I'll go first." That's my answer.

Q: As it happens, they aren't saying that!

Rajaram: But at the same time, we have to be very aware that, at first, we didn't know the consequences of the Green Revolution on our land, water, and the rest. We didn't educate the farmers on how they had to apply nitrogen; how much? Sometimes the farmer used a lot!

Naturally, that way, the water is going to be contaminated. But today we do know. The American Society of Agronomy itself knows all about crops, about soil. We are getting close to having an excellent simulation technology for all the things we can do, and that we have to do! Ultimately, if we don't educate our farmers to do things right, we are going to come out wrong.

Therefore I say this: I cannot accept this philosophy.

But I am a very convinced proponent that we have to protect our biodiversity, all the resources that we have, one way or another; and we also have to bring in the most advanced technology possible to be able to produce, while conserving the environment and soil and water. What doesn't contaminate! There is science!

We have learned something in 50 years. Yes, we polluted, but this was an oversight. No one knew! We talk about micronutrients in the soil: The more we have, the more we can grow. But we have to keep adding them to maintain a healthy, viable soil, and to not contaminate the environment.

So, let these people tell me: Who is the first of them to go because there is no food? Are they going to say the

FIGURE 2
Mexico Water Projects: The PLHINO and the PLHIGON

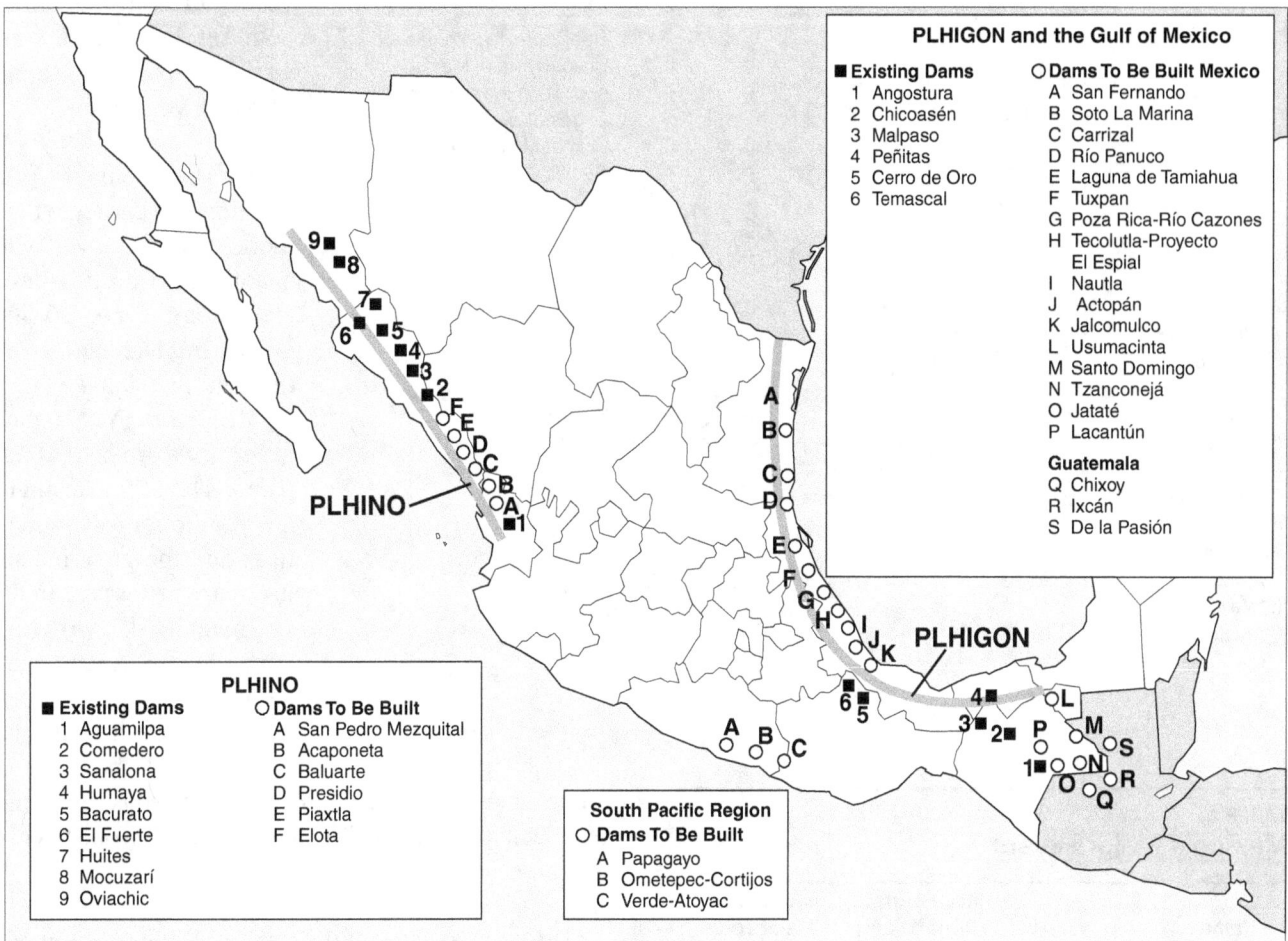

The PLHINO (Northwest Hydraulic Plan), and the PLHIGON (Northern Gulf Hydraulic Plan) were first proposed in the 1960s, and have been held up since then.

poor should die first? Everyone, including the poor, has the same right! The Catholic religion says that we all have the same rights, correct?

Q: Exactly! That is why we singled out the GLOBE report, because it is truly oligarchical thinking. It is very tilted to say: You cannot develop. It is like not having a right to exist.

Rajaram: We have to give opportunities to the poor. We must! We have a moral, ethical total obligation not to deny them. If we deny them, they are going to be the first to die, in some way or another. All the problems of disease are also problems of nutrition, in the main.

Q: Exactly! In the face of the greatest food crisis

ever, GLOBE's statements sound like a death sentence for those in our country and in the world who have no food.

Build Projects, Build the PLHINO

To produce what we need in the way of food, great infrastructure projects like the ones we are proposing, the PLHINO are needed, and also to activate the principles of the Green Revolution, which has nothing to do with the arguments of the Natural Capital document.

What do you think of creating these kinds of projects worldwide, and especially, the PLHINO for the northwest of the country?

Rajaram: I am very in favor of the PLHINO plan. I believe that this kind of project is going to substantially help us in the production of sufficient food for the entire

FIGURE 3
Mexico's Major Rivers, and 'PLHINO Rivers'

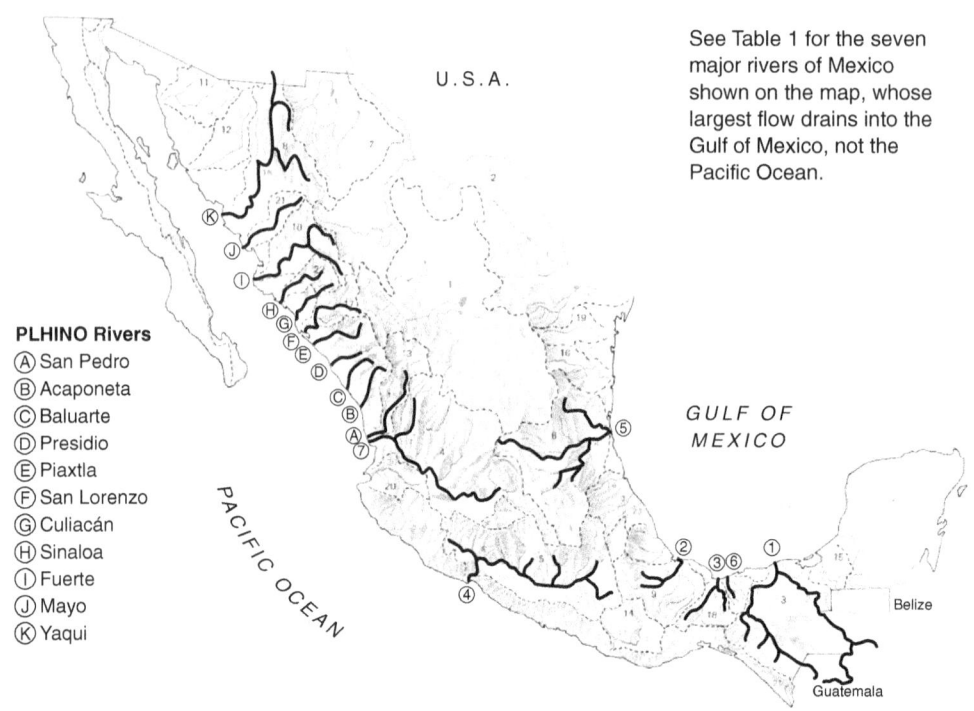

See Table 1 for the seven major rivers of Mexico shown on the map, whose largest flow drains into the Gulf of Mexico, not the Pacific Ocean.

PLHINO Rivers
- Ⓐ San Pedro
- Ⓑ Acaponeta
- Ⓒ Baluarte
- Ⓓ Presidio
- Ⓔ Piaxtla
- Ⓕ San Lorenzo
- Ⓖ Culiacán
- Ⓗ Sinaloa
- Ⓘ Fuerte
- Ⓙ Mayo
- Ⓚ Yaqui

EIR, 2007; INEGI data (Mexico)

TABLE 1
Mexico's Major Rivers

Name	Mean Surface Runoff (km³)	Runoff as % of Total
1) Grijalva-Usumacinta	115.5	29%
2) Papaloapan	44.7	11
3) Coatzacoalcos	32.8	8
4) Balsas	24.3	6
5) Pánuco	19.1	5
6) Tonalá	11.4	3
7) Santiago	7.8	2
Others	139.5	35
Total Mexico	**395.1**	**100**
—Empty into Gulf of Mexico	272	69
—Empty into Pacific Ocean	116	29
—Inland rivers	7	2

Source: CNA 2006 (Mexico).

country. It is going to be an example for other countries as well, of how to manage water.

At the same time, we need to look at the other implications. Remember that the PLHINO will be more or less along the coast, but there is also a mountain range.

I would like for us to be able to maintain the biodiversity all along this route, both for the animals, as well as for the natural Mexican vegetation.

Q: Of course! You mentioned earlier, that more technology will enable us to do this; less technology, no. With greater understanding of these things, right?

Rajaram: Yes, today perhaps we are better prepared: The Mexican engineers, agronomists, scientists, and the government itself, are better prepared.

Imagine if we had done this 50 years ago, perhaps a habitat would have been destroyed; but today we are better prepared and know how to do this. All we need is a government decision and a will on the part of everyone to collaborate.

Q: Our associates in the Pro-PLHINO Committee, who are working the most actively with farmers there—what would you advise them to do in pursuing the fight to get the PLHINO project done?

Rajaram: Naturally, we are a democratic country, and if our Congress, if our government, agrees, I don't know why should we have to have any fights in order to achieve it, because it is good for everyone. As they say in English, sharing the resources among all, for the good of all. This will be good for all.

However, I would say that in this sharing, we have to make sure that the resources or benefits don't stay in just one place without reaching other places, because we have to look after all the people, not only the farmers, but also the ranchers, who produce the best beef in Sonora.

Q: In the country, doctor!
Rajaram: We may have to look after the tequila producers, also!

Frontier Science

Q: There are important scientific research questions. For example, in developing desirable plant traits, and transferring a characteristic of one species to another, what about the work underway to upgrade rice from a C3 to C4 plant [higher-level carbon-fixing—ed.], so that it would share this characteristic which corn has, with respect to photosynthesis. What is to be said about this?

Rajaram: There are other genes which we could manage more easily. As an example: resistance to resins, high protein content—transfer this from one species to another. Add a colorant to help the assimilation of vitamin A, when it is one place, and not in another.

Many people think that we can convert all products into C4; in my view, that is too optimistic. I would like to keep it as it is. There's a lot to do within C4 or C3. Because, imagine, if we had a wheat plant which is C3, and we turn it into C4, it should also be adapted for tropical conditions. There are a lot of implications. We also need wheat in temperate climates.

There are many other things that could be done. I wouldn't like money to be spent on that now. Instead, we can increase, with good genes, the amount of lysine in the wheat, corn, or other crops.

Q: What about farming advancements—hydroponics, or farming without soil, farming in a controlled environment?

Rajaram: I agree. I think we could speak about this on a family scale. I don't mean that each family could harvest their own vegetables—very few could do that. Large-scale hydroponics to provide a lot of food wouldn't be very effective for cereals, but it would be for vegetables. Particularly if the vegetables could be produced at home, on the roof, it would be good, because it is very efficient, non-polluting. The water could be controlled, and little water is needed.

Also, with protected farming, under big greenhouses, flowers, tomatoes, cucumbers, or chili peppers can be grown. It is also very efficient. It's more efficient than when we do it in an open environment.

Q: What about rhizomes for wheat, this idea that the plant can be made to self-fertilize, by an ability to capture nitrogen? Is this something which is being investigated? Is it being done?

Rajaram: There was an investigation in Brazil, in the 1970s, by a plant scientist there. She did a lot of work trying to transfer the bacteria that form nodules in legumes, and she wanted to stimulate that characteristic in wheat roots. But I don't know what's being done currently. Perhaps biotechnology may open this frontier. If we could supplement something, because we have a lot of nitrogen in the environment, it would be very beneficial.

But this is something I call frontier science. Frontier science opens many, many possibilities, if we have the resources to do it. But I say that cautiously, because there are priorities. For me, the priorities are issues related to weather, because of climate change: high temperature, drought, floods, etc. These are the most important things biotechnology may help us to deal with, problems that we will face in 10 to 15, 20 years.

Q: For rice, Dr. Robert Zeigler has stressed this climate change concern, for example, in talking about everything that could be done to provide resistance to floods, drought, and salt. Much rice is produced in deltas, so if sea levels rise, we have to consider flooding, but also salt.

Rajaram: Here the problems are frosts; in the valley of Toluca.

Don't Patent Life-Forms

Q: In the days of Dr. Norman Borlaug, and Henry Wallace before him, there weren't patents for living organisms, and there was public funding for research. In this regard, we had the opportunity to attend, on July 18 of this year, the forum on "Reforms for Transforming the Countryside" in Irapuato, Guanajuato, organized by the Ministry of Agriculture, Livestock, Rural Development, Fisheries, and Food, whose subject was biotechnology and its applications to improve agriculture. The general call of the meeting was that, now that some patents are about to expire, we should use them for our benefit, to produce food, etc. What do you think about private companies being able to patent a form of life?

Rajaram: I don't agree. I'm not happy about big multinational companies patenting, or being able to patent, anything they want, like a gene or something; because these genes and these plants come from thousands of years ago, in which many people have worked to develop and maintain them. Thanks to that, we have today thousands of different varieties of corn in this country; and somebody coming along now and saying, "This is mine"—no, I do not agree.

I would like, although I know it's not possible, for

FIGURE 4

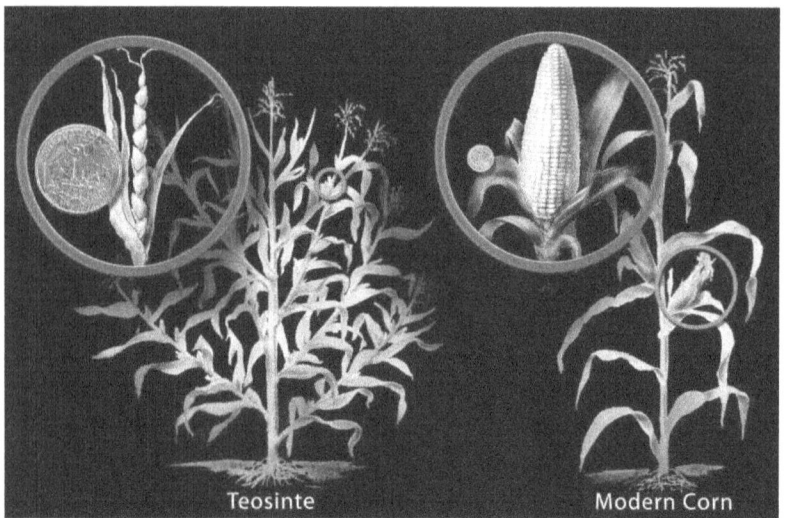

Teosinte — Modern Corn

NSF/Nicolle Roger Fuller

The ancestor of modern corn was the wild teosinte plant, in Mexico.

natural genetic resources to be available for everyone.

Let me put it another way: There are 26 letters in the English alphabet, and 27 or 28 in the Spanish alphabet, with the *ñ* and the *ll*. All this is basic, they are letters; it's like the gene. These letters are available; they are in the dictionary. Along with these letters, there are words, and these words are available for everyone in the free market. They are in the dictionary for everyone; they are free. But when a writer writes a novel, writes a book, those have different values: There's more of a market for one book than for another.

The private companies or the international governmental institutions should have complete freedom to use it and to make the best products with them. In the end, the farmer will decide which is good, and which is not. Those who make something better will sell more, but it has to be available.

What I hear today, is that somebody says, "I found this bacteria gene, and it's mine." No! This bacteria gene was already there, and somebody preserved it for a long time; or some link in the maize that Mexican farmers preserved that way over thousands of years. A farmer in the Middle East kept an offshoot of wheat; a species of potato in Peru or somewhere else; rice in South Asia. All these people have kept this for thousands of years. Nobody has the right to say, "It's mine." I would say that it sounds very radical for everybody to say, "We should protect," but, protect what? It is not yours to protect; it should be free.

That's why I'm very grateful for various interna-

tional centers, such as the CIMMYT, because they say that their germplasm is for everyone. Sometimes they sell it and we have to pay for it. That's not a problem, because international centers like the CIMMYT need to be maintained, because they have done such a great job for mankind. Dr. Borlaug was there; I was there. And yes, Henry Wallace's policy was fundamental for the CIMMYT to exist. I don't know where this man came from!

Q: Iowa.

Rajaram: I know, but I mean how he thought, how he managed to leave this heritage.

Q: That's because Henry Wallace's family was tied to agriculture, and since he was a child, he thought that it was a mistake that farmers took the biggest ears of corn, thinking that they were the best. He felt that it's not about size, but about quality.

In the vacation he took after the 1942 election, after helping Franklin Delano Roosevelt for three terms, to save the economy after the whole crisis of 1929, Wallace traveled to Mexico, in his own old car, because he wanted to get to know Mexico, because it was the land of corn. When he drove through the countryside, he realized that Mexico really didn't have the infrastructural and technological capacity to produce.

What surprised him—and this relates to the cooperation principle behind the Good Neighbor policy, which says: When your neighbor is doing well, you'll be doing well, too—is that, as he said, "I can't believe there is so much hunger so close to our home." Hence, his interest in increasing cooperation, and sending Norman Borlaug.

Rajaram: Well, he didn't send Norman Borlaug. That should be corrected. Norman Borlaug was selected by Dr. E.C. Stackman, a professor of pathology at the University of Minnesota, a very good professor. Norman worked with him, and Dr. E.C. Stackman and two other researchers were commissioned to do a study in Mexico in order to establish this collaboration that we are talking about, because the CIMMYT didn't exist at that time; it was the Office of Special Affairs, in coordination with the Mexican government, which authorized it.

But the idea came from Henry Wallace, and it was

the President who wanted this the most. The President was good—not all the American Presidents are like that—and he wanted to establish this kind of situation to help Mexico. It is exemplary, and out of this came the International Centers, many other projects funded by Rockefeller and Ford, and it was in this way that Norman was sent, along with another scientist specializing in corn, Edwin J. Wellhausen, and another specialist in potatoes, whose name I have forgotten, but he was an American, also.

They came, and they were young, but were very good working with Mexicans, and they all learned the language. That's why I learned the Mexican language! When I saw Norman, I said: "Wait, if he can speak the language, why not me?"

Q: Thank you, Dr. Rajaram, for your remarks, which will help people understand in more detail the true role of biotechnology in developing food production, and the role that we should have as scientists, researchers, politicians, students, etc., to help these projects get done.

Give us a last message for the youth, so that your words may help them to decide their future.

Rajaram: I would tell the youth who are in the university, or who graduated from the university and are already working, not only in agricultural science, but also in other sciences, or art, or geography, it doesn't matter which one—that they all must have a very broad vision. We can't look at agricultural science through a very little hole. We have to focus on having a very broad interaction. We have to be open to learning, much more, much more than we were taught in university. Broaden knowledge, and apply it. And work hard. Because we can be very intelligent, but we won't accomplish much if we are lazy. We have to work hard. But we also have to look after the family; I don't mean you should neglect the family. But you have to work, and work, and you have to apply science with a broad vision. And that way you will be successful.

The future of Mexico and of many other countries depends on their young people. And that's why I would like for them, once they have graduated from university, to get some training, which is good for applications, so that they can do good work.

They need to be well paid, also. Because if they are not well paid, how can they be expected to do good work? They have to earn a living, too.

Translated from Spanish by Valerie Rush

FIGURE 5
Wheat Yields, 1950-2004, in Mexico, India, and Pakistan

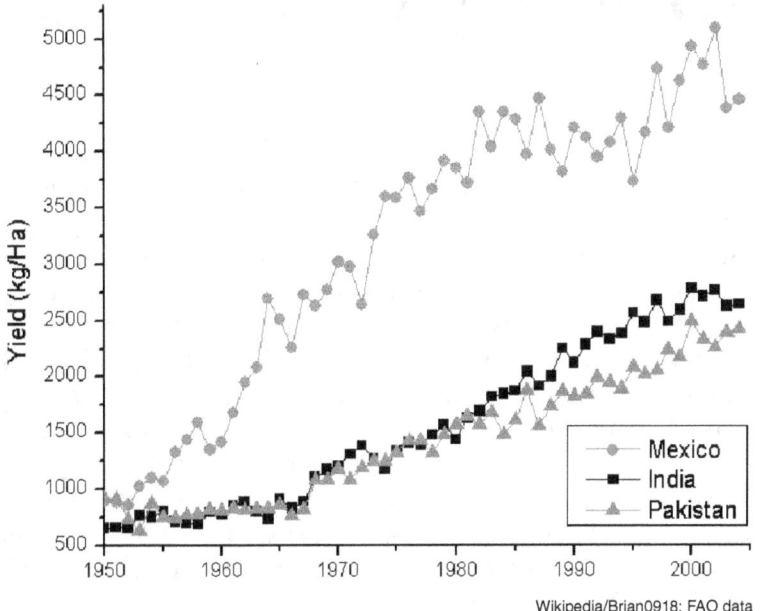

Wikipedia/Brian0918; FAO data

THE 1870S SHOWDOWN

America's Former Greatness And the World's Future

by Anton Chaitkin

A Spectacular Irony

The United States introduced to the world a modern way of life; "captured the lightning," and put nature's powers at humanity's service. The brightened world applauded America's inventions and the example of its skilled, well-paid producers. Its national dignity was that the common citizen could accomplish anything needed to solve problems, through genius and persistent work.

Following the Union victory in the Civil War, with active government nurturing of industrial growth, the success of this American outlook was rapid and startling; there were limitless technical accomplishments. Newly powerful, the USA extended the hand of friendship to rising nations, and showed them the way to overcome British imperial stratagems blocking their industrialization.[1]

In a highly coordinated fashion, leaders everywhere adopted the American nationalist strategy as the guide to the formation of their own countries' power. Thus did the anti-imperial American Revolution blossom in the emergence of Russia, Germany, Japan, and in the national movements that led to the modern states of China, India, Ireland, and elsewhere.

But the London imperial center and its Wall Street offshoot at length gained power over American industry and strategy. By the 21st Century, the USA had surrendered its world-shaping way of life, closed its productive industries, and thrown itself into a suicidal Anglo-American casino economy and permanent war scenario.

In recent months, sentient Americans have grown increasingly alarmed at the prospects for survival as the U.S. government and the bankrupt "Western" system have lurched toward thermonuclear confrontation with Russia and China.

Together with India and some other developing countries, these supposedly adversarial nations are building nuclear plants and planning for fusion energy, resuming a bold space program, constructing high-speed rail lines to cure backwardness.

We must face the brutal truth: that these new leading nations are moving the world to a peaceful, cooperative order, and are thus resuming the old American strategy for human progress, while the Americans, ignorant of their heritage, have abandoned their successful existence.

Revolutionary Philadelphia

You are about to read of stirring events occurring largely in Philadelphia. Now a post-industrial shadow of its former vitality, that city was at the center of world strategic action, from the American Revolution up to a

---

1. The U.S. envisioned a world of skilled, modern nations. U.S.-Russian cooperation in particular could hasten this development, and bring about peace, with a "land-bridge" connecting by rail the whole Western Hemisphere and through Eurasia. After the Russians built their Trans-Siberian Railroad, emulating Lincoln's Transcontinental Railroad, Tsar Nicholas II proposed bridging the Bering Strait. The Chinese have recently revived the project for a Bering Strait tunnel as a proposal for action.

master nature's secrets, and to rapidly increase common living standards. His image, and his city of Philadelphia, became associated with the idea—the demand—that these goals should guide a nation's policy.

It began with Franklin nurturing his partners and young "Junto" followers as a revolutionary movement for industrial progress and political change. This same movement continued to act in Philadelphia as the headquarters of the American Revolution and the continuing center of *economic nationalism*.

What then was the National Idea inherent in the U.S. Constitution, written in Philadelphia, and in Alexander Hamilton's credit system, executed through the Philadelphia-based Bank of the United States?

To grasp its meaning, to see into the minds of America's founders, you must place that idea in its real context: bloody political conflict.

The global contest between the republic's power and that of its enemy, the old imperial financier oligarchy, underlies all serious issues of U.S. history, from the Revolution to the present day.

Franklin's city first took off in the 1820s. Nicholas Biddle (the president of the Bank of the United States) and Mathew Carey (Irish insurgent leader, a Franklin

Portraits of Thomas Edison by Abraham Archibald Anderson (above) and of "Benjamin Franklin Drawing Electricity from the Sky," by Benjamin West (right). Franklin's republican concepts shaped the work of the American System thinkers discussed in this article, notably including Edison.

shattering climax in the decade of this narrative.

Long before Benjamin Franklin ran the Secret Committees of the Continental Congress, procured the essential foreign support for the Revolution, and supervised the writing of the Declaration of Independence, he was world-famous as the pioneer of the science of electricity. He had decisively broken with British imperial philosophy; he had gone to England itself, and had roused and guided the inventive initiatives of anti-imperial Britons in the Industrial Revolution.

The success of Franklin's life work helped spread a new concept of republicanism: a popular ambition to

protégé, who became the prophet of American nationalism) together guided development-minded investors and local and state governments to begin commercially mining American coal for the first time; to build a huge network of canals to pour out the new fuel into shops and cities; to forge iron, and to erect the most advanced machine-building shops.

U.S. President John Quincy Adams and Congressional leader Henry Clay worked closely with them, raising protective tariffs, and assigning Army engineers to begin planning the first American railroads, which were funded by the Bank of the United States.

Philadelphians of genius and humanity founded the Franklin Institute in 1824, to envision, plan, and test new technologies and to educate an inventive working population. Physicist/surveyor Alexander Dallas Bache (1806-67), Franklin's great-grandson, became the Institute's research chief and coordinated with Germany's Carl Gauss a global network of pro-republic scientists (Bache's friends took control of the Harvard and Yale science programs before the Civil War). Mathew Carey mentored immigrant economist Friedrich List, who left Pennsylvania as a U.S. consul, consolidated German states under a tariff union, and started up the first railroads in Germany.

Philadelphia and the state government financed creation of the Pennsylvania Railroad. Engineering and scheduling discipline from former military personnel, and the interchangeable parts system introduced at U.S. armories, would make the Pennsylvania Railroad the world's largest company by the 1860s. The Baldwin Locomotive Works was the biggest supplier to the railroads and the world's most important capital goods producer; it trained several generations of creative skilled workers.

Geometry of the Showdown

Two distinct sides faced each other in the global struggle for the world's future, from 1871 to a direct collision in 1881.

Within the USA and in each of its allied developing countries was a core grouping of political-economy strategists, industrialists, scientists, senior military officers, nationalist politicians, and certain labor organizers. The creative souls comprising the informal "national party" were united by a passion to free mankind

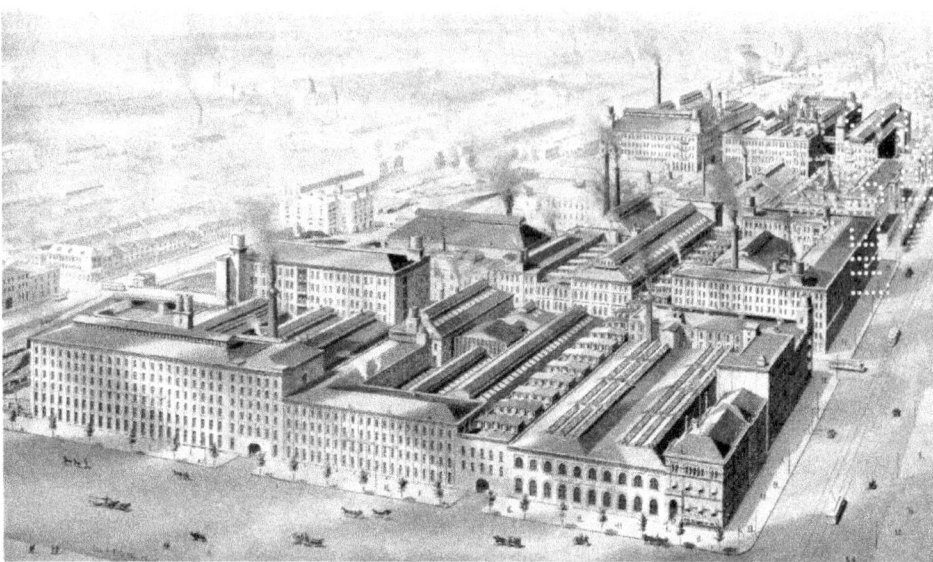

History of the Baldwin Locomotive Works from 1831-1913

The huge Baldwin Locomotive Works in Philadelphia, around the beginning of the 20th Century. Baldwin was the world's biggest supplier to the railroads.

from ignorance, backwardness, and poverty, and from the British-centered imperial financial system and its perpetual wars.

Against them was the oligarchy: the Anglo-Dutch monarchy, private bankers, and aristocrats, the permanent royal institutions such as British intelligence operating through state and private channels; and their wealthy, anti-national allies within each country and inside the USA (Wall Street, Anglophile academics, and press). The British used extortion, assassination, and riots. They employed anarchist and other provocative movements—forerunners of the 21st-Century "color revolutions" and blind terrorists.

The leaders of the two sides, in the time-period of the action we shall describe, are identified in the accompanying box.

The Civil War's mass slaughter ended with the murder of President Lincoln. But his nationalist measures were still in effect, and the victorious Union persisted in plans to remake the world. The U.S. demanded and collected monetary damages from the British for sponsoring the Confederate war machine, but the central objective was to build a new economy whose power would ensure peace and safety.

High tariffs sheltered the birth of an American steel industry. The government donated free land to western settlers, and Lincoln's Agriculture Department gave scientific advice to the farmers.

Lincoln and Congress had funded two transconti-

U.S. Strategic Leadership

The main players in the narrative are in bold.

Henry C. Carey (1793-1879), economist, global strategist vs. British imperial system; son of Mathew Carey; procured 1860s high tariff for industrialization

Figures Associated with Carey: Morton McMichael, publisher, Phila. mayor, originator of the 1876 Centennial Exhibition; banker **Wharton Barker**; *Irish revolutionaries*: William Carroll, physician, leader Clan na Gael; John Devoy, chief strategist Irish republicanism; Robert Ellis Thompson, economist; Terence Powderly, head of Knights of Labor, created Greenback-Labor Party. *Ambassadors to Russia*: Cassius M. Clay, Kentucky anti-slavery activist, U.S. ambassador to Russia (1861-62, 1863-67); Andrew Curtin, Penn. governor in Civil War, ambassador to Russia (1869-72); George H. Boker, Phila. municipal leader, ambassador to Russia (1875-78); Wickham Hoffman, wartime aide to Gen. William T. Sherman, led U.S. embassy in Russia (1877-83)

Carey Family Firm: Carey's brother-in-law Isaac Lea, scientist, publishing partner of Mathew and Henry Carey; **Henry Charles Lea**, Isaac's son and publishing partner; collaborated with Wharton Barker to elect President Garfield

The Industrial League, founded 1868 by Carey's lobbyists Morton McMichael, Henry C. Lea, Joseph Wharton and William Sellers

"Philadelphia Interests": owners of Penn. Railroad and other rail, steel, coal, oil, machine industries, funded Franklin Institute, American Philosophical Society, Univ. of Penn. as auxiliary strategic institutions—Thomas A. Scott (president Penn. Railroad, 1874-80), Andrew Carnegie, William J. Palmer, Joseph Wharton, Mathias Baldwin, and Matthew Baird of Baldwin Locomotives, machine designers William and Coleman Sellers, Samuel M. Felton

Joseph D. Potts, pioneer oil industry developer for Pennsylvania Railroad

Jay Cooke, main private banker for U.S. government, promoter of industrial development projects for Philadelphia Interests

Benjamin Silliman, Jr., chemist, scientific founder of U.S. oil industry

Thomas A. Edison, sponsored as inventor by Philadelphia Interests

George F. Barker, mentor to Edison; University of Pennsylvannia physicist/physician, Franklin Institute research chief, close to Carey's political circle, president of American Association for the Advancement of Science and American Chemical Society, secretary of American Philosophical Society

Gen. William T. Sherman

James G. Blaine, Secretary of State (1881, 1889-92)

James A. Garfield, President (1881)

Foreign Pro-Development Leaders

Russia: Alexander II, the "Tsar Liberator," modernized Russia, freed the serfs; his brother Grand Duke Constantine Nikolaevich, pro-American reformer, Navy head; Grand Duke's aide-de-camp **Capt. Leonid Semetschkin**; Dolgoruky family; **Dmitri Mendeleyev**, chemist who created the Periodic Table of the Elements; Nikolai Shishkin, ambassador to the U.S. (1875-80)

Germany: Chancellor Otto von Bismarck; Wilhelm von Kardorff, leader of Carey-affiliated nationalist party; William T. Mulvany, Irish engineer, founded German heavy industries, economic nationalist; **Emil Rathenau**, industrialist

Japan: leaders of 1868 Meiji Restoration, many of them Carey collaborators

Anti-National U.S. Oligarchs

John Pierpont (J.P.) Morgan, son of London banker Junius Morgan

Anthony Drexel, Phila. banker

John D. Rockefeller, oil monopolist

Roscoe Conkling, U.S. Senator (N.Y.), head of Wall Street financier faction within Republican Party

Chester A. Arthur, Conkling's operative, later Vice President, President

Cornelius Vanderbilt, rail and stock plunderer, sponsored Rockefeller

August Belmont, N.Y. representative of Rothschild bankers and London oligarchs

nental railroads that were to link the farmers, their machinery suppliers, and urban markets. The Union Pacific to the San Francisco Bay was completed in 1869. The Northern Pacific then began construction from Wisconsin to Seattle, aiming to build the West and mutually develop America, Russia, and Asia.

The U.S. economy immediately exploded in size, inventiveness, and ambition. This growth was largely

Baldwin Railroads: The Harmony of Interests

A visitor to Philadelphia today can stroll a short distance from downtown to Matthias Baldwin Park, the former site of the Baldwin Locomotive Works' main plant. Foreigners may be moved to contemplate there, the now-vanished instrument for industrialization of their own countries. The firm made 70,000 locomotives for the world, from the 1830s to the 1950s.

Baldwin workers were the highest paid in that era. The piece-work policy—a standard rate for each unit produced—was used for higher output, but never employed to cut wages. Many Baldwin men owned their own homes; about half the city's population were workers' families living there.

The plant owners knew that a worker earning higher pay was more valuable to them. Building a better world, they were proud of the American high-wage model as the natural legacy of their anti-colonial Revolution. Workers and owners both had a stake in the firm's success; both sought the improvement of society for their children and grandchildren.

This "Harmony of Interests" (the title of Henry C. Carey's influential 1851 book) worked well when the USA pursued its mission of "elevating while equalizing the condition of man throughout the world." But neither good wages nor profitable, productive investments could be left to the whims of private financiers and to credit control by the trans-Atlantic empire. In 1844, Baldwin's employees were prominent in a demonstration for Presidential candidate Henry Clay, who demanded protective tariffs and the return of a national bank for development. It was on behalf of men such as these locomotive builders that the 1860 Presidential candidate Abraham Lincoln pledged himself to nationalist economics.

Baldwin workers were among those who looked to unions for protection in bad times, as when "free trade" policies caused economic disaster. There was a strike at the Baldwin plant in 1860, and another in 1893. Workers struck in 1911, when J.P. Morgan moved for control of the company; the strikers' leaflet, entitled "Shall Morgan Own This Country?", warned that the lord of Wall Street was making Americans his slaves. But from the time Abraham Lincoln came in, as long as his national policies endured, there was satisfaction in the Baldwin ranks.

A boy of 16 could be taken on as a Baldwin apprentice in a skilled trade, such as machinist, blacksmith, molder-founder, boilermaker/sheet-iron/coppersmith, pattern-maker, ornamental painter, or in drafting/designing. Families of Baldwin workers, and poor parents or orphan guardians, avidly sought these positions for their sons. The pay was nominal, but the owners looked out for the apprentice. At completion of the five-year term, a bonus was paid, and the young man was secure among the elite of qualified workers.

The partners who owned Baldwin—some of whom had been apprentices—were each experts in some vital aspect of the enterprise, such as design, supply, production or the technical needs of the customer railroads. There were no speculating financiers as absentee owners. Foremen (skilled workers) guided the shop floor action. There were no managers, none of those non-producing bosses scorned as dead-weights on the backs of workers and owners.

This was the best of the American way of life, and it was shaping the world. The Russian nobleman Mikhail Khilkov worked and learned as a Baldwin machinist in 1860-61. In 1895, he was appointed Russia's Minister of Ways of Communication, to build the great Trans-Siberian Railway—with Baldwin locomotives and Pennsylvania steel. Prince Khilkov was known in Russia as "the American."[1]

---

1. John K. Brown, *The Baldwin Locomotive Works, 1831-1915: A Study in American Industrial Practice* (Baltimore, Johns Hopkins University Press, 1995). Brown's excellent study is the source of much of this section.

driven by the formation of new heavy industry within Pennsylvania, led by Franklin's Philadelphians.

The Pennsylvania Railroad, Baldwin Locomotive Works, and Andrew Carnegie jointly applied the new Bessemer process to American steelmaking. They built railroads and bridges out of steel—not with the weaker iron previously used—from the Midwest to the Rocky Mountains.

Production growth in the new industry was spectacular (**Table 1**).

TABLE 1
Growth of U.S. Production

	Steel (tons)	Steel Rails (tons)	Iron Rails (tons)	Coal (tons)*	Petroleum (gallons)
1869	31,000	8,000	521,000	33,000,000	177,000,000
1881	1,588,000	1,210,000	436,000	86,000,000	1,162,000,000

*For metal-making and railroad fuel

Source: Fred J. Guetter and Albert E. McKinley, *Statistical Tables Relating to the Economic Growth of the United States* (Philadelphia: McKinley Publishing Company, 1924), pp. 31-32, 36.

The United States had come out of the Civil War with the world's largest army and most advanced navy. Now the growth of U.S. industrial power was the glaring fact at the center of world politics. America was fast outstripping Britain, and was aiding others to do the same.

This reality was reflected in the 1872 visit to Philadelphia by representatives of the Emperor and government of Japan. The city's establishment published an anonymous pamphlet ("Diary of the Japanese Visit to Philadelphia") describing the manufacturing plants, shipbuilders, and other sites they toured. It proclaimed that before the United States went to aid Japan's development, Japan was closed to world commerce, in self-defense against the European empires: "the least concession ... to the foreign trader" had previously brought in "that aggressive policy, that arrogance, and grasping spirit of monopoly which have ever followed the British footfall on foreign soil," forcing Japan to close up "as a means to preserve its national and political autonomy."

Baldwin Locomotive president Matthew Baird made all the tour arrangements. The city's report-pamphlet described the enthralled visitors at the Baldwin plant. Tameyossi Hida, Chief Commissioner of Japan's Public Works Department, inspected drawings and models: "With one model of a valve action Hida was so much interested that it was with difficulty he was induced to leave it, turning back repeatedly to test its action, until he had evidently grasped, not only the principle, but all the details; and when he was promised a duplicate of this model, his satisfaction was unbounded."

Philadelphia was only one stop on the 1871-73 world tour led by Prince Iwakura, seeking to modernize Japan; and Japan did not officially announce an alliance with the United States. But during the tour, the Finance Ministry set up an institute to train Japanese economists in the American System tradition of Henry Carey and Friedrich List, and the government would itself publish Carey's 1858 *Principles of Social Science*. (The "Iwakura Embassy" tour is well known in Japan; but the world is generally unaware of its central connection to the nationalists' hegemony within the USA.)

Prince Iwakura and Cabinet ministers met with Philadelphia banker Jay Cooke and worked to prepare a $15 million loan for Japanese development. Chief of the Northern Pacific Railroad project, Cooke negotiated with the Japanese for Asian connections as part of a projected global belt of railways, canals, and shipping operations intended to vastly upgrade the economy and power of many sovereign nations.

The Enemy Strikes

From the 19th to the present century, the names Morgan and Rockefeller have been identified with Wall Street's power over American life. JPMorgan Chase was created in 2000, merging JPMorgan and Co. and the Rockefeller family bank Chase Manhattan. As the largest U.S. bank, it led the recent years' wild derivatives speculation and subsequent bailouts.

There is in general no competent opinion about Wall Street and its power. This is because the public, however critical of these unelected rulers, does not have a clue as to their origin—how and when they took charge of ruining our industries and destroying our national sovereignty.

Their global war against America's national mission is still going on. In the intervening years since the 19th-Century showdown, they and their imperial sponsors have flipped the power of the United States onto the enemy side of the conflict.

In 1872, New York's Wall Street financial district was already a power, as an adjunct and instrument of the City of London oligarchy. Wall Street's operators had grown rich from slavery, financing the export of Southern slave-produced cotton to England. They had turned a cold shoulder to Lincoln during the Civil War—for borrowed funds, the government had to rely on small-denomination bonds which Jay Cooke and his sales force sold to patriotic citizens.

After the Union victory, Cooke was the banking linchpin for the vast nation-building enterprises of the Philadelphia industrialists. Wall Street was powerful, but did not rule America, and its mother, the British Empire, saw doom approaching, riding American trains.

Banker Jay Cooke was the linchpin for financing the Philadelphia industrialists after the Civil War. London drove him into bankruptcy in 1873.

In 1872, a crippling attack against Cooke and the Philadelphia nationalists was quietly being readied. This two-pronged assault would propel the Morgan and Rockefeller interests into the status of British viceroys over America.

Banking War...

At age 20 in 1857, the American-born J.P. Morgan had joined his father, Junius Morgan, in London's Peabody, Morgan and Co. This private bank was an operational arm of the America-handling strategy of Queen Victoria and her Prime Minister, Lord Palmerston. The young Morgan later moved to New York as the British firm's American representative. During the Civil War, having paid a substitute to go into the Union Army for him, he speculated wildly in gold against the dollar and sent intelligence to London. Morgan financed the purchase of 5,000 obsolete rifles from an Army arsenal for $17,000 and their re-sale to a field general for $110,000.

This sleaze did not hamper his reception by elite East Coast Anglophiles. Morgan was not just anybody: He was the blood-proud maternal grandson, namesake, and protégé of John Pierpont (1785-1866), through whom Morgan had a "romantic" link to the history of Anglo-American intrigue.

Grandfather Pierpont was a propagandist for the pro-British "Essex Junto" in Massachusetts, and third cousin of Aaron Burr, the New York political boss and U.S. Vice President. After Burr killed Alexander Hamilton in 1804, Pierpont moved to South Carolina and became an employee of Burr's family and the tutor to Burr's grandson. The next year, Burr put himself in the British service to attempt the break-up of the United States, and came south to work out the scheme with his son-in-law, Joseph Alston, Pierpont's employer. Burr designated Alston to be his successor as the "emperor" of the western lands that the Burr-Britain combination could seize, and his grandson, Pierpont's ward, was to be next in line. But Burr was arrested for treason, secession was deferred, and the boy died. Thus for Pierpont, Burr's grandson would not be the dreamed-of North American emperor—but his own grandson would be.

Philadelphia was the political and industrial heart of the USA that was reshaping the world against the British Empire. On June 30, 1871, Junius Morgan dissolved his son's New York firm and put J.P. into a partnership with Anthony Drexel in Philadelphia, as London's representatives to attack the American nationalists in their home base.

In 1872, Drexel, Morgan and Co. circulated libels against the solvency and honesty of Jay Cooke's bank and the Northern Pacific Railroad he was building, "predicting" an anti-Cooke panic. The lies were printed in the Philadelphia *Ledger*—controlled by Anthony Drexel; and in the London *Times* (*Ledger* editor George Childs was an "intimate house guest" in London with *Times* financial editor H.B. Sampson). The lies were reprinted as leaflets, passed around in banking circles in Europe and America. Scandals were simultaneously gotten up against the completed Union Pacific, frightening Congress away from further supporting Cooke and the construction of the Northern Pacific.

Drexel, Morgan demanded that the government award to them, rather than to their rival Cooke, the purchase and resale of a new Federal bond issue. Drexel, Morgan formed a bond-buying syndicate with Wall Street's Levi Morton, representing Morton's London partner, Sir John Rose; Junius Morgan in London; and the British Empire giant, Baring Brothers. The gravely weakened Cooke was driven to form his own syndicate with the British Rothschilds. President Ulysses S. Grant, who was pro-development, but financially befuddled, and counted Anthony Drexel as a friend, had his Treasury Department compromise in January 1873,

J.P. Morgan: "I have come to the conclusion that neither my firm nor myself will have anything to do, hereafter, directly or indirectly, with the negotiation of securities of any undertaking not entirely completed...."

splitting the $300 million between the two camps.

The *New York Times* reported March 5, 1873, that the Bank of England had lost a large chunk of Cooke's deposits to swindlers. British bankers froze Cooke out of the money markets. The Barings and the Rothschilds (the latter Cooke's syndicate partners), talked down the value of the U.S. government bonds Cooke was then marketing.

On Sept. 18, 1873, Jay Cooke and Co. collapsed, detonating a worldwide crisis and a depression of many years' duration. Northern Pacific Railway construction was halted. The panic-stricken New York Stock Exchange closed for a week.

Uniquely among banking firms in America, Morgan made over $1 million profit in the 1873 crisis. The previous year, anticipating victory over the American nationalists, the firm had begun construction of a new headquarters palace in New York, by far the largest and most sumptuous office building on Wall Street. In the wake of the crisis, the London-Wall Street axis demanded "hard money" and, in 1875, pushed through passage of the Specie Resumption Act, breaking down Lincoln's Greenback system.

London was now in charge of U.S. government financing.

Drexel, Morgan became J.P. Morgan and Co. (called informally the House of Morgan). As the firm began taking over U.S. railroads, J.P. Morgan explained the basic investment principle for Wall Street which he had "learned" in the crisis his firm had brought about: Seize control of industries, but build nothing new. In a letter to his father dated April 29, 1874, he wrote, "I have come to the conclusion that neither my firm nor myself will have anything to do, hereafter, directly or indirectly, with the negotiation of securities of any undertaking not entirely completed..." (quoted in Ron Chernow, *The House of Morgan* [1990], p. 37).

...And Oil War

The world's modern petroleum industry was born when the little Pennsylvania Rock Oil Company in Venango County sent a sample of the crude oil seeping out of the ground, to Yale University chemistry professor Benjamin Silliman, Jr., to analyze its potential use for lighting and lubrication. Silliman's thorough 1855 report to the company confirmed that the substance could easily be distilled into a valuable product, could be accessed by drilling wells, and was identical to the oil springs found in Russia and Persia. The resulting rush of speculative drillers quickly made northwestern Pennsylvania's Oil Region the center of an enormous new industry.

After the Civil War, ambitious Army veterans poured in, pumping oil for big money, but facing chaos in shipping their product. The Pennsylvania Railroad created a subsidiary, the Empire Transportation Company, to organize the Oil Region's logistics. Empire president Col. Joseph D. Potts was a passionate patriot. His family had owned Valley (iron) Forge and General Washington had rented his uncle's house for the Revolutionary Army headquarters. Potts himself had organized all transport for the state government in the early period of the Civil War.

Potts now quickly developed pipelines, coordinated oil shipments over many previously disconnected rail lines, and put a fleet of oil-carrying ships on the Great Lakes.

As the previous generation had midwifed the birth of America's coal industry, the Pennsylvania Railroad and the Empire Transportation Co. now guided the formation of a strategically vital new source of wealth for mankind.

Enter John D. Rockefeller. His father, William Avery Rockefeller, was a fake-elixir salesman and bigamist who explained, "I cheat my boys every chance I get. I want to make 'em sharp." At age 20 in 1859, John D. went into the commission grocery business in Cleveland, Ohio. He hired substitutes to serve in his place in the Union Army, and in 1863, accepted the proposal of the monarchy-worshipping English chemist Samuel Andrews for a Cleveland partnership to refine oil from neighboring Pennsylvania. Rockefeller & Andrews boomed. John's brother William set up a sales office in New York City, and the family merged their destiny with the top Wall Street financiers, speculators, and exporters.

Rockefeller and his partners incorporated as Standard Oil in 1870 and the next year declared a 40% dividend to stockholders. At the beginning of 1872, Wall Street bankers and speculators poured in millions to stake Rockefeller for his mission: Get volume-based shipping rebates from railroads, so he could undercut, destroy, and buy out other refiners—and then move in to wreck the Philadelphia-based nationalists, Wall Street's mortal enemy.

Cornelius Vanderbilt, in particular, backed Rockefeller for this pirate mission. Vanderbilt used his control of the New York Central and other railroads, which he had grabbed

One-dimensional British view: John D. Rockefeller, in Puck Magazine (1901)

Real American history: William Vanderbilt continues his father Cornelius' use of Rockefeller to destroy American industry (Daily Graphic, 1879).

through audacious deceit, stock fraud, and the bribery of an entire legislature.

Thus armed by Wall Street money and its railroad owners, Rockefeller, in 1872, coerced the Pennsylvania Railroad and many oil firms into a secret agreement for a cartel to be called the South Improvement Company. Those who immediately signed on were supposed to get rebates; all others would be crushed and eaten. Though the oil producers revolted and the Pennsylvania legislature prohibited the deal, Rockefeller used the mere threat of this power to bully all other Cleveland refiners into submission. Producing no crude oil, Rockefeller bought up refineries in New York, then in Philadelphia and Pittsburgh.

His engorged company was the first industrial trust in America. Standard Oil now looked out upon the Pennsylvania refiners as its prey, and it circled around the Pennsylvania Railroad and its Empire subsidiary, which kept it from its meal.

But the nationalists persisted, despite the Morgan-induced 1870s depression, and in the face of Rockefeller's pressure.

The Empire Transportation Company erected new oil infrastructure, operating 1,500 tank cars, 500 miles of pipelines, and storage facilities for a substantial portion of the nation's production. Baldwin was able to keep its full workforce going with locomotive orders for Russia. Andrew Carnegie built the world's most modern steel mills and bridges. William J. Palmer constructed rail lines on the Great Plains and founded cities and industries along the Rocky Mountains.

The Future Human Race at the Centennial

Philadelphia made itself the site for the Centennial Exhibition of Arts, Manufactures, and Products of the Soil and Mine, to celebrate the 100th anniversary of the 1776 Declaration of Independence. It would show off man's newly acquired productive powers, and display the republic's astonishing advances since its Civil War victory. It was the particular project of Henry C. Carey. His close associates, such as Mayor Morton McMichael and the Franklin Institute, successfully organized the city to prepare this world's fair and got the U.S. Congress to sponsor it.

Visitors from all over the world (about 10 million admissions were recorded) came to the Exhibition from May to November 1876, riding special Pennsylvania Railroad tour trains to 200 buildings representing all the states and many nations. They saw the greatest array of inventions and industrial and agricultural devices ever shown, from ingenious models, to gorgeous locomotives, to giant machines propelling the exhibits.

From these American displays, visiting foreigners, wheels and axles spinning in their minds, went home to help their reform-minded leaders elevate their nations' power, as the Americans were doing. The world was suddenly on a course of progress never before imaginable.

Henry Carey set the tone. He was there to meet and confer, with the Centennial Exhibition's unofficial "battle manual": his famous 1876 pamphlet attacked the opium-pushing British Empire's cheap labor "free trade" system as an attack on Christianity and civilization, in contrast to the protected American high-wage system of industrial success.[2]

Henry C. Carey, economic advisor to President Lincoln, was the theoretician of the American System of national industrialization, battling British free trade and slavery.

(In view of the battle described in this article, the thoughtful person will have strongly conflicting emotions when visiting Fairmont Park's Memorial Hall, built in 1876 to house the art gallery of the Centennial. Today, a guide there uses the ingenious detailed model of the entire exhibition to explain the background of that world-shaping event.)

We will now meet three distinguished foreign visitors to the exhibition: a Russian scientist, Dmitri Mendeleyev; a German industrialist, Emil Rathenau; and a Russian military officer, Capt. Leonid Semetschkin. We will follow them and their American colleagues through the global showdown, to the disaster and promise which ensued.

To Illuminate the Darkness of the Whole World

A scientist is a man who does something where no question of making money is involved. Understand? And two scientists who deal with each other are dealing about something, about anything which does not concern money.[3]

—Dmitri Mendeleyev, answering a peasant

Seven years before this trip, Mendelev had fired scientific imaginations and re-ordered the world's chemical ideas with his Periodic Table of the Elements.

Why had he come? He wrote that "sympathy towards the Americans has long been urging me to their country.... [When] it became known ... that the exhibition in 1876 would be in America, I decided to travel there.... Everyone expected to see many original, purely American mechanical inventions in Philadelphia ... the products of American technological genius....

"European civilization has been expressed in its strongest and best manifestations in the United States, discarding many of the old harmful traditions, and exerting an effort to develop the individuality, and ... actual social freedom.... The fame of America ... in-

2. Henry C. Carey, "Commerce, Christianity, and Civilization, versus British Free Trade. Letters in Reply to the London Times" (Philadelphia: 1876).

3. Paraphrased in Daniel Q. Posin, *Mendeleyev: The Story of a Great Scientist* (New York: McGraw-Hill, 1948), p. 180.

Russian scientist Dmitri Mendeleyev, portrait by Ilya Repin (1885). On the right is Mendeleyev's map of the "Pennsylvania Oil Regions," from his book "The Oil Industry in Pennsylvania and the Caucasus" (1877).

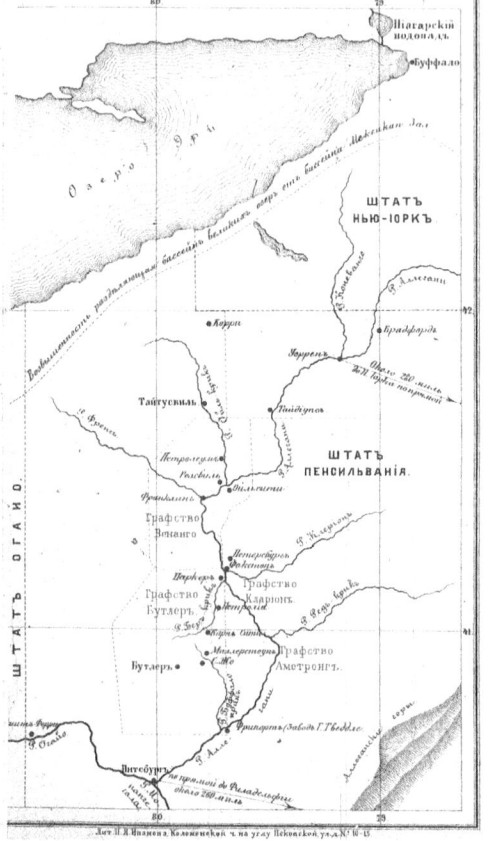

creased especially in the period [of its Civil War], because slavery was a strong stain on the free institutions of the States. I wanted to see myself... the peculiarities created by American institutions ... (and I desired) to get to know first-hand the development of the oil industry in America, especially in Pennsylvania, which is supplying the whole world with its lighting oil."[4]

J. Peter Lesley guided Mendeleyev's technical consultations. A pioneering researcher in oil, coal, and steelmaking for the nationalists, Lesley ran the American Philosophical Society in that era, and was a kindred soul to Mendeleyev's genius. The Russian met American scientists, toured new refineries, and scouted the oil fields.

Mendeleyev certainly saw the Centennial display of American inventor George Brayton's giant internal combustion engine, fueled by petroleum. Five years later, the Brayton engine would drive its first vehicle— a weapon of war directed against the British Empire.

Mendeleyev wrote that he was briefed on the situation of the oil industry by a representative of the Empire Transportation Company. In Empire's own building at the Exhibition, beautiful working models—ships, pipelines, the railroad tank car (their invention)—illustrated how the company had organized America's oil transport. Their briefing for Mendeleyev reflected the impending full-scale war for survival.

Mendeleyev, like Tsar Alexander II, saw America and Russia as sharing a common destiny of leadership for mankind's benefit. He wrote:

"A large part of [the world's] petroleum is extracted in the state of Pennsylvania in America. The Caucasus alone could compete with America in natural riches....

"Separated by history and distance, the North American States and Russia diverged in much—whence, however, is also their mutual sympathy. In the future these countries, therefore, would need to divide among themselves the benefits of the oil field and the right to illuminate the darkness of the whole world."

He warned of the danger posed by anti-national forces: "at the beginning of 1872, *The South Improvement Company* became a monopolist not only at home, but also on markets abroad, undermining the activity of other oil producers...."[5]

Returning to Russia to begin its petroleum development, Mendeleyev pushed for full-scale industrialization—a fight over Russia's future which would grow increasingly hot over the next five years.

By the end of the exhibition in November 1876, Rockefeller's monopoly was closing in. He paid spies

---

4. Dmitri Mendeleyev, *The Oil Industry in Pennsylvania and the Caucasus* (St. Petersburg: 1877), quotations translated by Pavel Penev.

5. Ibid.

EIRNS/Anton Chaitkin

Model of the Centennial Exhibition at Fairmont Park, Philadelphia. "The Centennial Exhibition of Arts, Manufactures, and Products of the Soil and Mine," celebrating the anniversary of the 1776 Declaration of Independence, was the particular project of Henry C. Carey. Visitors from around the world, among them Dmitri Mendeleyev, Emil Rathenau, and Capt. Leonid Semetschkin, were inspired to similar achievements in their own countries.

and traitors to give him precise guidance for strangling target companies, as Ida Tarbell revealed in her classic work, *The History of the Standard Oil Company* (1904).

The Pennsylvania Railroad and the Empire Company struck back in January 1877. Empire went into the refinery business, competing directly against Rockefeller, and pulled its tank cars out of servicing Standard refinery areas.

Wall Street, now increasingly ruled by Britain's J.P. Morgan, backed Rockefeller to issue an ultimatum to the Philadelphians in the Spring of 1877: He would ship absolutely no freight over the Pennsylvania Railroad unless Empire sold off its refineries.

Pennsylvania Railroad president Tom Scott defied the threat, so Rockefeller closed his refinery in Pittsburgh and other places uniquely served by the Pennsylvania RR. Vanderbilt loaned Rockefeller the cash to buy 600 new tank cars, which might travel over his New York Central Railroad. Standard Oil began buying up all available petroleum, and drastically cut prices for refined products wherever Empire was doing business.

Scott responded by radically cutting shipping charges for Empire, and reduced passenger fares to at-tract customers from Vanderbilt's lines; Potts built and bought more refineries.

The Pennsylvania Railroad lost millions of dollars and had to lay off workers and cut wages, as other depression-ravaged railways were doing. A strike broke out against the railroad. Under cover of this defensive action, mobs destroyed thousands of PRR freight cars and over 100 locomotives, and torched its train stations. No Rockefeller facility was attacked, and no strike occurred against Vanderbilt's rail lines. (Anglophile and Wall Street-influenced historians, including leftists, have shown no curiosity about the relation of the sabotage during the Great Railroad Strike of 1877 to the stupendous battle then being waged for control of the nation.)

Scott capitulated. Empire Transportation sold all its assets and closed down completely.

Rockefeller soon consolidated control over U.S. oil production. Cornelius Vanderbilt died in 1877 worth $100 million. His son sold railroad shares through J.P. Morgan to British aristocrats, and his granddaughter married the Duke of Marlborough. J.P. Morgan took over most American railroads. By the turn of the century, Morgan would seize most of the country's heavy industry.

Mankind Captures Franklin's Lightning

Emil Rathenau came to the Centennial to study America's technological progress. He left Philadelphia inspired by the treasures he saw in Machinery Hall, and committed to introducing American methods into German industries. It is likely, but not certain, that Rathenau met Thomas A. Edison there in 1876. Several years later, under extraordinary circumstances, the two men would form a partnership that shaped modern society.

Young Edison displayed at the Exhibition the telegraphic technology he had designed for the Philadelphia interests; his genius had landed him in the middle of their bitter strategic war.

He was born into that fight, in a way. His Canadian father, Samuel Edison (1804-96), was a leading militant in the 1837 rebellion against British rule. Written up for treason against the Empire, Sam had fled across the border into Michigan with armed forces in pursuit. His son Thomas was born in 1847, and Sam—a hater of Wall Street and the idle rich—was his counselor for the next half century.

Thomas Edison worked on trains as a youth, and became an operator of the telegraph system accompanying the rail line. He was an inventive telegrapher in New York in 1870, when his already celebrated talent was rescued from Wall Street by the Philadelphians.

William J. Palmer, a Medal of Honor-winning cavalry officer and a partner to Scott and Carnegie, was then building the Kansas Pacific Railway out to Denver as an adjunct to Lincoln's first transcontinental line. Palmer's railway needed telegraph technology that could outflank Vanderbilt's Western Union monopoly. Edison was then developing a means of sending multiple messages simultaneously both ways on a wire, but Wall Street and London systematically bought up and suppressed or misused such innovations.

So Palmer set up the Automatic Telegraph Company in New York, sending his railroad-construction assistant, Edward H. Johnson, to manage the firm. They hired Edison to be a full-time inventor, with a $40,000 advance that set him free to soar.

By 1874, Philadelphia's nationalist elite had adopted Edison. Franklin Institute leader George Barker became his scientific mentor and guardian.

Vattenfall AB

Emil Rathenau, founder of the Deutsche Edison-Gesellschaft (later known as Allgemeine Elektricitäts-Gesellschaft, AEG), and Thomas Edison meet in Berlin in 1911. The partnership between the two men electrified the world and shaped modern society.

In March 1876, they backed his move to Menlo Park, N.J., where an independent "invention laboratory" was built for him under the supervision of his father; Philadelphia's Edward Johnson was, from then on, Edison's chief executive assistant and publicist. A few months later, Edison was displaying his multiplex telegraph, when Rathenau and other advocates of progress came to the Centennial.

The following year, Edison invented the phonograph, the world's first device to record sound and play it back. The Pennsylvania Railroad ran special trains of visitors to Menlo Park to see the phonograph exhibited. Professor Barker arranged to have the sensational machine introducd at a meeting of the National Academy of Sciences. A phonograph party for Washington dignitaries was held by Sen. James Blaine's niece; there Edison recited and played back a ditty pointedly offensive to Blaine's enemy, Wall Street's Sen. Roscoe Conkling. The party moved on to the White House to let the hapless President, Rutherford Hayes, play with the novelty.

In July 1878, Barker took Edison out West during a solar eclipse to try out Edison's new "tasimeter" (to measure infrared radiation from individual stars). On this trip, the professor explained the development of electrical science since Franklin, and reviewed recent halting attempts to produce light from electricity. Barker proposed that Edison take on this challenge, taking him to Connecticut in September, to inspect an outdoor arc light (a flame between electrodes) and an electric generator powered by a water wheel.

From that moment, Edison was on fire. He conceived of the task in universal terms: Electrically heat some material inside a glass to make it glow without burning up; power an unlimited number from one source ("divide the light"); make gas lights obsolete with an efficient, steam-driven electric generator; and invent the hundreds of devices to connect homes and factories to a central station.

But how could this development work be paid for, when Edison's Philadelphia backers were staggering financially? He would need publicity, to win public support for better leverage with Wall Street. A few days after returning from Connecticut, he announced that he had invented the electric light, that he would light and heat the cities, that he would power up elevators, sewing machines, and cooking stoves.

A *Washington Post* item on Oct. 17, 1878, conveys the anxiety of the London-Wall Street axis: "Edison's bruited discovery of a practical method of subdividing electric light has caused a panic in the London gas stocks and seriously depressed gas stocks in New York and Montreal. To have made gas directors tremble in their boots is glory enough for Edison, even if his machine doesn't work."

The very next day, the same newspaper reported the formation of the Edison Electric Light Company. It was controlled by J.P. Morgan and by Morgan-dominated Western Union.

On Oct. 30, Morgan cabled to his brother-in-law Walter Burns, who handled intelligence for Junius Morgan: "I have been engaged ... on a matter which is ... most important ... not only ... to the world ... but to us in particular.... Secrecy at the moment is so essential that I do not dare put it on paper. Subject is Edison's Electric light—importance can be realized from the ed-

itorials in London *Times* & other papers & the effect upon gas stocks which have declined from 25-50% since rumors [of] Edison's success... [T]his matter needs careful handling if anything comes of it. It is not entirely certain. I shall do nothing until it is—but when that time comes ... we must be prepared to strike...."[6]

In December 1878, J.P. Morgan and Anthony Drexel came to Menlo Park to negotiate for global rights to the as-yet-uncreated light and power devices. Edison got funding; Morgan got the power to limit or stifle his work.

Edison labored to perfect his system, while the enemy churned out propaganda against him. A British Parliament special committee took testimony that widescale electric light was impossible and electric power would be dangerous in public hands. The military intelligence think tank, Royal United Service Institution, was assured on Feb. 15, 1879, "It is ... easily shown by the application of well-known scientific laws that .... a sub-division of the electric light is an absolute *ignis fatuus* [will-o'-the-wisp]."[7] The *New York Times* re-ran the British line that Edison's project was impossible.

In 1879, Edison patented a carbon-thread incandescent lamp that could burn for 40 hours, and soon made a bulb rated for 1,500 hours. He patented hundreds of devices essential to his child, the electrical industry.

But J.P. Morgan blocked light bulb manufacture. Edison sold stock in the Morgan-controlled Edison Electric Light Company (EELC). He and Edward Johnson created the Edison Lamp Company to make bulbs. Morgan financed one power station for a small section of New York City, but he blocked any further power plant construction, until the "free market" showed electricity was in demand. With public acclaim behind him, Edison and the Philadelphians got up a brutal fight on the EELC board, loosening Morgan veto-power for a time.

Edison reached out to American municipalities, and they issued their own bonds to construct the first generation of America's central power stations—12 by 1884, 58 by 1886. His team now rushed to electrify other continents, as will be seen below.

_____

6. Quoted in Paul Israel, *Edison: A Life of Invention* (New York: John Wiley & Sons, 1998), p. 174.
7. William Henry Preece, Electrician of the General Post Office, "The Electric Light," lecture Jan. 31, 1879, p. 97, in *Royal United Services Journal*, Vol. xxiii, No. xcix (London: Royal United Services Institute for Defence Studies, 1879)

American Alliances vs. the British Empire

Tsar Alexander II had sent Russian warships during America's Civil War to stay for months in the ports of New York and San Francisco, to warn the British and French that they would have to fight Russia if they intervened on the side of the Southern slave-owners. Seeing that the British were arming Confederate cruisers for attacks on American merchant vessels, Russian officers in New York had drawn up their own plan for "privateering" against the British.

In November 1876, the last month of the Centennial Exhibition, Britain began threatening war against Russia over the Balkans crisis. The Tsar's brother Grand Duke Constantine, Russia's General Admiral, sought to revive the privateering idea and consulted with his aide-de-camp, Capt. Leonid Semetschkin, who had co-authored the 1863 privateering plan. Semetschkin was then in Philadelphia, having been sent to conduct Russia's naval exhibit at the 1876 Centennial Exhibition. The Russian consulted with his hosts at the Centennial and drew up a new plan, congenial to American laws and strategy. It was approved by the Tsar, but the Balkans crisis cooled and it was shelved. Two years later, put into action by American and Russian strategists, the plan would cause a political earthquake.

Archives of the Russian Navy

Capt. Leonid Semetschkin arranged the purchase of U.S.-made warships in case of war with Britain.

A group known as the Penn Club had been created by Henry Carey and his friends, just before the Centennial, as a locus for entertaining and private discussions with distinguished visitors such as Captain Semetschkin, Dmitri Mendeleyev, and Emil Rathenau.

Carey's political lieutenant, banker Wharton Barker,[8] chaired the Penn Club during the Centennial. Reflecting Carey's influence over relations with Russia, Barker was also the banker for the Russian government group organizing that country's participation in the Philadelphia Exhibition; he and Semetschkin became close friends.

Carey was still brilliant at 82. The Penn Club continued, for a half-century-younger generation, his famous weekly strategy discussions known as the "Carey Vespers." Over the next few years, until Carey's 1879 death and beyond, Philadelphia's Carey circle moved the world's decisive events.

The Careyites and their foreign collaborators largely drove the spectacular policy revolutions and resultant modernization of Germany and Japan. They revived and reorganized Ireland's political war for independence from British tyranny. They created the Greenback-Labor Party to fight against London-Wall Street economic sabotage. They made the Knights of Labor the most effective mass workers' movement (including women, jobless, blacks, and immigrants) to teach economics and undercut enemy-controlled anarchism.

This privately directed, interconnected global activism crested in 1878.

That year, Chancellor Otto von Bismarck rushed Germany's shift from British-dictated "free trade" to America's government-guided industrialization,[9] as demonstrated at the Centennial and presented by Carey's German representatives. In Germany, paralleling the Philadelphia interests, an Irish engineer with bitter memories of British misrule, William T. Mulvany, had moved to Germany, developed the Ruhr region's coal and transport, and collaborated with the Carey machine to give Bismarck political leverage for his nationalist coup.

The Iron Chancellor put through protective tariffs, created modern railroads, directed banks to invest productively, and provided for workers' pensions. Overnight, Germany became a world power, joining the United States to surpass Britain industrially.

At that time, two steel-nerved Irish émigrés at Wharton Barker's side steered the trans-Atlantic Irish underground, as heads of the Clan na Gael organization: the Irish republican John Devoy and Philadelphia physician William Carroll. Devoy and Carroll had minuscule resources, but they covertly visited Ireland and England and ran a vast network for intelligence, fundraising, and gun-running. They shaped support for political nationalism in Ireland around the figure of Charles Parnell. They outsmarted and undercut the

---

8. No relation to George Barker. Wharton Barker's family bank, Barker Brothers, was in part a financial vehicle for Bethlehem Steel owner Joseph Wharton, Wharton Barker's uncle.

9. See Helga Zepp-LaRouche, "The American Roots of Germany's Industrial Revolution," [[*EIR*,]] Sept. 12, 2008. [[http://www.larouchepub.com/eiw/public/2008/ 2008_30-39/2008-37/pdf/38-55_3536.pdf]]

British Secret Service agents who were provoking terrorism.

A war crisis now reappeared between Russia and Britain. Barker, Devoy, and Carroll discussed with Russian Ambassador N.P. Shishkin the prospects for an Irish uprising, within a potential joint American-Russian war to finish off the British Empire.

The Russian Cruisers

In the Spring of 1878, as Russia had defeated the Ottoman Empire in the Russo-Turkish war (1877-78), enraged British oligarchs flooded the press with alarms about the Russian Menace. The London *Times* wrote on March 25, 1878, "*England must either declare war for the purpose of diminishing Russian prestige, or inflict upon her some humiliation....*"[10]

Tsar Alexander II decided to go ahead rapidly with the purchase of several advanced warships built in the United States; they must be out of port before war commenced with Britain. The Tsar met with Captain Semetschkin on April 8 and ordered him to go ahead immediately.

The story of the purportedly secret mission leaked out. On April 20, Wickham Hoffman, the American chargé d'affaires in St. Petersburg, reported to Washington: "the Hamburg steamer *Cimbria* chartered by the Russian government, left Port Baltic ... with 66 officers and 600 sailors of the Russian Navy to man the steamers built for the Russian government at Philadelphia. I know of no reason why Russia or any other power should not build war vessels in the United States, if it sees fit, but in view of the present threatening relations between Russia and Great Britain, I have thought you might wish to be advised of this circumstance...."[11]

Commissioned by Russia, Wharton Barker had created a make-believe Alaskan steamship company and ordered four ships to be built for it at Philadelphia's

Banker Wharton Barker, political lieutenant of Henry Carey, negotiated the sale of U.S. warships to Russia; he was also the architect of James A. Garfield's campaign for the Presidency.

William Cramp & Sons shipyard. Barker was to take the ships when completed out beyond U.S. territorial waters and turn them over to Russian commanders, who would install the guns and ammunition bought by Barker and ferried out by other vessels.

American and British newspapers exploded with coverage as the *Cimbria* arrived on April 28 in Southwest Harbor, Maine. British naval attaché Adm. William Gore Jones came up from the U.K. Embassy in Washington; he was repulsed in two attempts to board the *Cimbria* and inspect its manifest. The British nervously watched the ship from the dock until it departed for Philadelphia.

On May 16, Semetschkin gave Barker a formal purchase order of $400,000 for the steamship *State of California*, whose refitting from commercial vessel to war cruiser was then being completed. The next day, Admiral Gore Jones offered Cramp & Sons $500,000 for the *California*, and soon futilely raised his offer to $600,000. British Ambassador Edward Thornton advised the Foreign Office and the British Navy of the ship's sale to the Russians through Wharton Barker.

John Devoy and William Carroll leaked to the New York and British press that thousands of Irish-Americans, having pledged to join the Russian service, were already drilling at the Canadian border and would march on Nova Scotia or New Brunswick in the event of war. The nationalist press in Ireland followed the progress of the Semetschkin episode and exulted in Britain's distress.

Amid mounting British hysteria, William Gore Jones got himself into the Cramp & Sons shipyard disguised as a workman, affecting an Irish brogue. But a Russian officer spied him out, and he was ejected by the shipyard watchman; the incident was publicly mocked in Washington.[12]

10. Quoted in Frederick Douglas How, *The Marquis of Salisbury* (London: Isbister & Co., 1901), p. 127.

11. Wickham Hoffman to Secretary of State Evarts, April 20, 1878, quoted in Leonid Strakhovsky, "Russia's privateering projects of 1878," *Journal of Modern History*, VII (1935), p. 26.

12. Augustus C. Buell, *The Memoirs of Charles H. Cramp* (Philadelphia: J.B. Lipincott Company, 1906). The entire episode of the Russian cruisers is told in the Cramp Memoirs.

The *State of California*, the *Columbus*, the *Saratoga*, and a fourth ship expressly built for the Russians, were commissioned as warships in the Russian service on July 15, 1878, under the names *Europe, Asia, Africa*, and *Zabiaka* (the last, whose name means "mischief-maker," was the fastest cruiser in the world at that time).

The British backed down from their war threat. It was the British, not the Russians, who had been humiliated.

Wharton Barker was in Russia in Summer 1879. With Alexander II and Grand Duke Constantine, he reviewed the Russian fleet, including the new ships he had put into their service, and they decorated him with the Order of St. Stanislaus. The Tsar told Barker that during the Civil War he had protected America by sending the Navy to U.S. ports, "because I understood that Russia would have a more serious task to perform if the American Republic, with advanced industrial development, was broken up and Great Britain left in control of most branches of modern industrial development."

Now the triumphant republic was awakening the world's suppressed productive forces. U.S. minister Wickham Hoffman in St. Petersburg facilitated huge orders of Baldwin locomotives, which boosted Russian economic power.

The danger that the American idea posed to the Empire had been spelled out in the English newspaper *The Spectator* (Jan. 11, 1873). A strengthened Russia might remake poor, thinly populated Persia (Iran), so that its role as a buffer for British India might end: "Persia might in ten years be restored by Russian engineers . . . to become once more a garden in which a great population might grow rich. . . . Water once secured— and securing water is in Persia an engineering affair only—there is no country in the world with higher natural advantages for agriculture, stock-breeding, and mining enterprise than Persia. . . ."

Yet the British were well aware that as the 1870s ended, this U.S. strategic outlook was concentrated in the private hands of a money-poor nationalist faction, and was not, as it had been with Lincoln, the bold public policy of the Presidency.

This the Philadelphians now set out to remedy.

Taking the White House

It was in their *Penn Monthly*, edited by Henry Carey's disciple Robert Ellis Thompson, that the Carey

Official portrait of President James A. Garfield, by Calvin Curtis (1881). Garfield warred with Wall Street and was assassinated in 1881, after only a few months in office.

circle in May 1879, first proposed the Presidential candidacy of Congressman James A. Garfield. The magazine's publisher, Wharton Barker, declared him to be a man of "high principle" and the best man for the White House. (A Civil War general and former Greek teacher, Garfield had devised a unique proof of the Pythagorean Theorem while discussing geometry with other Congressmen in 1876.)

In a December 1879 letter, Barker proposed to Garfield that he should run for President. Barker had just returned from Russia as a man of some notoriety, and was publicly seen as continuing the work of Henry C. Carey, who had died in October.

Barker and Garfield met in early January, and agreed that Barker would proceed in his efforts to secure the 1880 Republican nomination for Garfield.

The Carey circle now put into play the political apparatus associated with the Industrial League they had created in 1868. Two hundred Philadelphia leaders signed a manifesto issued by a meeting of prominent Philadelphians at the home of Carey's nephew, Henry Carey Lea. This started up the National Republican League, aiming to break Wall Street's hold over their party and national politics.

The three main candidates were unacceptable:

• Senator Blaine's supporters were too wedded to the Party;

• Secretary of the Treasury John Sherman (brother of Gen. William T. Sherman) "served the creditor class";[13]

• and Wall Street ran former President Ulysses Grant's third-term candidacy through Roscoe Conkling's Stalwart faction Republicans.

Barker calculated that none could get enough delegates at the Republican Convention to take the nomination, and he surmised that the three camps' mutual bitterness would make his "dark horse" candidate acceptable.

Though certain secret operations were only revealed later, Barker was widely discussed at the time as architect of the Garfield campaign. Yet his role has been erased by the national historical amnesia spread by London and Wall Street.

After getting Garfield to explain how he had become a member of the elite Cobden Club without sharing its pro-British "free trade" purpose, Barker crisscrossed the country, very quietly setting the springs of action.

He procured New England opposition to Blaine as unelectable.

When the Carey team secretly swung the Philadelphia Republican machine out of its lock for Wall Street/ Grant, a crisis arose. Treasury Secretary John Sherman spoke at a dinner held by the Philadelphia Stock Exchange. Wharton's father Abram Barker, who was president of the Exchange, evidently boasted of his son's plans to Sherman.

Sherman then cleverly begged Garfield to make the nomination speech for him at the forthcoming Convention—without telling Garfield that his secret was out. Accepting Sherman's entreaties, Garfield told Barker he could not betray Sherman by his own candidacy. Barker assured Garfield that his friends could do more for him than he could himself, and plunged back into operation.

The 1880 Republican National Convention convened on June 2 in Chicago.

The Carey team had arrived well in advance to make arrangements. Among their delegates were Wharton Barker, Henry Carey Lea, Robert Ellis

Sen. Roscoe Conkling, head of Wall Street's Stalwart faction of the Republican Party, depicted by cartoonist Thomas Nast. President Garfield destroyed Conkling's career, and soon after, Garfield was assassinated.

Thompson, at least two other members of their Penn Club (Henry Reed and Samuel Pennypacker), and the Pennsylvania Railroad's counsel, Wayne MacVeagh, acting as Barker's chief lieutenant. Some of Carey's Irish nationalists attended as spectators and cheerleaders.

Barker directed paid squads in the galleries and on the floor to applaud whenever Garfield arrived for a session. At one juncture, Senator Conkling put through a resolution compelling delegates to swear they would support the party's nominee, then introduced another that the convention should expel the three delegates who had just voted "no." Barker prodded Garfield to speak, and his squads cheered when he finally rose. Garfield's stirring defense of freedom of conscience against party loyalty won the point and the convention roared its approval.

Barker's nationwide contact network performed on schedule, and all of Barker's calculations proved accurate. A deadlock held through 33 ballots, Garfield staying eligible with the one vote prearranged from Philadelphia machine boss W.A. Grier.

Supremely confident, Barker left Chicago for Russia

13. Wharton Barker, "The Secret History of the Garfield Nomination," *Pearson's Magazine*, May 1916.

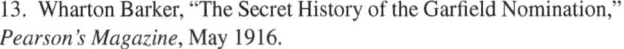

Franklin Institute

Locomotive 60000 on display at the Franklin Institute. This experimental machine, built in 1926, was the company's 60,000th locomotive. Baldwin produced huge number of locomotives for the Russian market, including during the post-1873 Morgan-induced depression in the United States.

prisoned and exiled Dublin Fenian newspaper editor through whom Carroll and Devoy regularly sent American funds to the Irish Republican Brotherhood (IRB); and John O'Connor, who, under assumed names, had for many years dodged British arrest as the chief channel of IRB communications within the British Isles.

Carroll later explained what ensued:

"...it was decided to issue an appeal to the Irish Nationalists of the United States, as American citizens, to vote against the English policy of Free Trade, through which Irish industries had been destroyed and which if not defeated would ruin those of America.... [The plan was put before] Chester A. Arthur, the candidate for Vice-President who promptly pronounced the appeal hopeless, [but with this] opinion Marshall Jewell, chairman of the Republican National Committee (former Ambassador to Russia 1873-4) and Mr. Barker differed, and the appeal, written in crisp, concise and convincing terms by Prof. Thompson appeared in 15 places in one day in the *New York Herald*; was placarded over the dead walls of New York and widely circulated elsewhere; all at Mr. Barker's expense. The response was the election of Garfield and Arthur...."[14]

As they were then stirring millions of first- and second-generation Irish in America to support their struggling brethren back home, the Philadelphia leaders prevailed on many of them to depart from their traditional support for the (pro-"free trade") Democrats and vote for Garfield.

The Irish were decisive in the November election. Garfield won the popular vote by only 9,000 out of the 9,000,000 national total. New York's 35 electoral votes

during the deadlock, to help plan the industrialization of southwestern Russia/Ukraine—coal, iron, steel, and railroads. In a July 6 letter to the Russian Foreign Ministry, he wrote of "the common work of Russia and America, namely the dismemberment of the British Empire."

On the 34th and 35th ballots, Wisconsin, and then Indiana, shifted their votes to Garfield as programmed, and a stampede on the 36th nominated him.

Blaine released his supporters to Garfield, turning the tide, and Garfield would make the nationalist Blaine his Secretary of State.

Sherman ceded his support to Garfield after President Hayes, following Barker's prompting, had urged his Treasury Secretary to do so.

The Wall Street faction was mollified by putting Conkling's New York operative Chester Arthur on the Garfield ticket for Vice President.

Several months before the convention, Robert Ellis Thompson had included Clan na Gael chief William Carroll in the plan. After the nomination, Dr. Carroll brought into Wharton Barker's banking office two visiting Irish revolutionary heroes: John O'Leary, the im-

---

14. Ibid.

gave Garfield the victory, with his margin of 21,000 out of 1,100,000 ballots cast in that state.

The Government in American Hands

Unease grew in New York and London prior to Garfield's inauguration. Could their Stalwarts, defeated for the Presidency, still control the U.S. Treasury?

Senator Conkling was demanding the post of Treasury Secretary for his ally, New York banker Levi P. Morton—Morgan's syndicate partner back in 1873.

The *New York Times* reported (Jan. 2, 1881) that President-elect Garfield had offered to make Morton Secretary of the Navy. But "Gen. Garfield's declination to give him the Secretaryship of the Treasury was caused by the fact that Mr. Morton is ... the senior ... member of a leading banking-house in London and New-York, which house has been a party in all the great syndicates for the placing of government loans, and [he is] particularly associated with all the banks and bankers in this country and Europe."

As a Congressman, Garfield had opposed syndicate financing in favor of bond sales to the people. Now he said he wanted no Wall Street man at Treasury.

James Garfield took office on Friday, March 4, 1881.

On Saturday, Robert Lincoln, son of the murdered President, was sworn as Secretary of War, and Wayne MacVeagh, Wharton Barker's convention lieutenant, came in as Attorney General.

Then on Sunday, the *New York Times* attacked Russia's "settled ingrained policy of aggression" in Central Asia; this threatened the Indian Empire—would Britain have to give up "hard-won Kandahar"?

On Monday, March 7, James Blaine, outspoken opponent of the British Empire, became Secretary of State; Minnesota protectionist William Windom took over the Treasury; and anti-Ku Klux Klan Louisianan

Library of Congress

James G. Blaine was an outspoken opponent of the British Empire, and Secretary of State in the Garfield Administration.

William H. Hunt became Secretary of the Navy, with a mandate to swiftly upgrade U.S. naval forces.

On March 10, a telegram informed Barker that the Tsar had ordered the acceptance of his concessions to help industrialize southern Russia, now that a government so favorable to his viewpoint was in place in Washington. A creative younger generation was beginning to work toward Mendeleyev's vision of a powerful Russia, taking its rightful place beside its American ally. The 31-year-old railroad developer Sergei Witte would soon emerge to lead Russia's progress out of feudalism, as an open advocate for the economic nationalism proving its success in America and Germany.

On March 13, nine days after Garfield's inauguration, Tsar Alexander II was blown up by a member of the nihilist movement that was notoriously co-owned by the British Empire and the Russian black nobility.

A global Anarchist Congress had assembled that Summer in London, where Prince Kropotkin would brag to 700 anti-national terrorists about the continuing murder campaign against the Russian government (*New York Times*, July 20, 1881).

The frightened successor, Alexander III, moved his residence out of St. Petersburg.

But Garfield moved straight ahead.

World Power

Two days after the Tsar's assassination, Blaine announced that the State Department would organize and plan U.S. participation in the International Congress of Electricity in Paris later that year.

Blaine appointed as American Commissioners for the event the Franklin Institute's George Barker (Edison's mentor); and George Gouraud (who was William J. Palmer's agent and fellow Medal of Honor recipient, and European manager for Edison); along

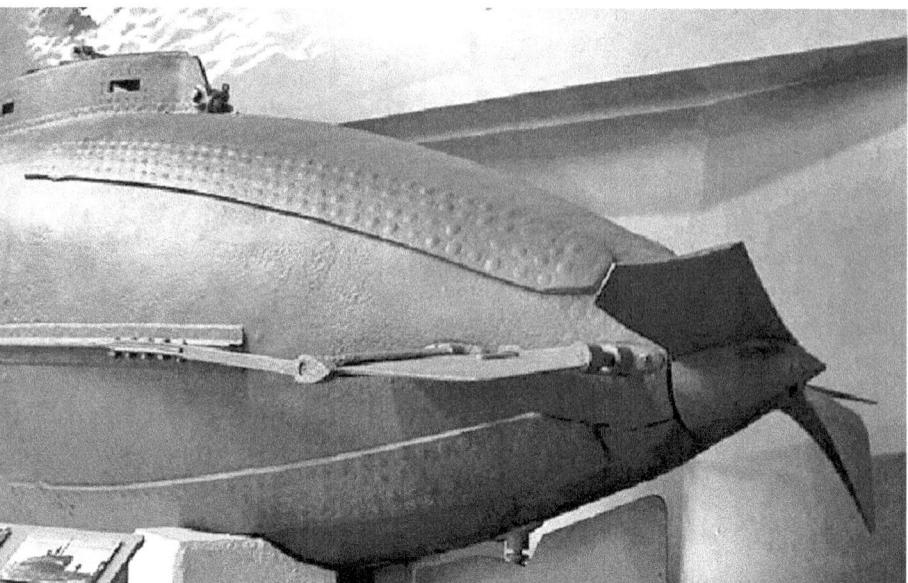

The Fenian Ram was the first modern submarine, designed by John Philip Holland (left) for use by the Fenian Brotherhood against the British. It was tested for combat duty in New York Harbor during the Garfield Administration, to the loud protests of the British government.

with State Department and U.S. military officers.

Paris streets and public schools were "magically lighted" that August, to celebrate the harnessing of electricity, this wonderful source of power. It was under U.S. government sponsorship that Germany's Emil Rathenau met Professor Barker in Paris and began a close friendship and partnership with Thomas Edison.

Rathenau got Edison's patents and the loan of Edison's power-plant engineer William Hammer. His German Edison Company (later known as Allgemeine Elektricitäts-Gesellschaft, AEG) now raced to electrify German society and industry, and the world economy. He built the electrical grids of Madrid, Warsaw, Genoa, and Buenos Aires, and brought power to Brazil, Chile, Mexico, and much of Western Europe.

Rathenau put electric power into St. Petersburg and street cars into Moscow. Later, he and his son Walther worked with Count Witte to build up Russia's own electrical industry, and AEG would electrify the Trans-Siberian Railroad.

Edison created other partnerships for light and power in Argentina, Cuba, Canada, Australia, China, Japan, India, South Africa, England, France, and Italy.

Confronting Britain in South America...

Wharton Barker proposed a Western Hemisphere customs union to Garfield before his election, and to the new President and Secretary of State when he met with them in April 1881. Just as Friedrich List's tariff union (the Zollverein) first brought together Germany's disparate states, the U.S. should negotiate a common shield to protect the wages and rising industries of both North and South America, against British domination and cheap-labor looting. This must be coupled with respect for national sovereignty and a drive for peace.

The Garfield Administration adopted this outlook and went into action in South America.

Peru had exalted ambitions, encouraged by Lincoln and Carey's nationalists: to create advanced machine, mining, and steel industries and ports. Peru had nationalized its nitrate deposits, raw material for the world's gunpowder. Planning a national rail grid that would extend to Brazil and begin industrializing the continent, Peru had hired California construction strategist Henry Meiggs, who built from the coast inland and up the Andes Mountains. When he died in 1877, the unfinished line was by far the world's highest railroad.

The British demanded absolute control over South

American finance and resources. They determined to exterminate Peru as a nation. Two successive nationalist Peruvian Presidents were assassinated, in 1872 and 1878.

Britain set a trap for the region. Nitrate deposits extended across the border into Bolivia and Chile. Chile was also pursuing some development ambitions— Meiggs had built railroads there as well. The British supplied Chile with arms and officers. The British trading company W.R. Grace, based in Lima, Santiago, and London, supplied Peru with arms and advised its government. The three neighbors were manipulated into a land and minerals conflict. Chile invaded Peru in 1879, with seven British Navy ships patrolling the coast. By mid-1880 Chilean forces occupied Lima, and Peruvian minerals were being sold off to pay British bondholders. Before Garfield and Blaine intervened, U.S. diplomats allowed Britain's representatives to dictate American acceptance of this mayhem.

Blaine resolved to deploy any aid necessary to protect Peruvian sovereignty and end the war. On May 18, 1881, Garfield nominated Stephen A. Hurlbut, Lincoln's tough counterintelligence specialist, as ambassador to Peru. By that time, the global strategic conflict had become a brutal face-off inside the United States.

…and in New York

Two years earlier, William Carroll, John Devoy, labor leader Terence Powderly and their Irish republican "skirmishing fund" had spent $18,000 funding a new super-weapon aimed at the Royal Navy: Irish émigré inventor John Holland built the first modern submarine, a 19-ton 4-man boat powered by a 17-horsepower Brayton petroleum engine (as displayed at the 1876 Centennial Exhibition). It fired dynamite-laden torpedoes.

With Garfield in the White House, the vessel (nicknamed the "Fenian Ram") was taken to Hoboken, N.J. and put into New York Harbor to be tested for combat duty. The first successful dive took place to spectators' amazement in June 1881. The British Consul in New York protested to the Treasury representative, the Collector of the Port of New York, demanding government surveillance of the project. But the Administration viewed the submarine as a private experiment and left the Fenians free to pursue it.

Political dynamite was then exploding around Wall Street.

The Collector of the Port wielded great patronage, and enough financial power to take on Wall Street. New York's Congressional representatives were usually given their own choice for the office. After being denied control over the Presidency or the Treasury Department, Stalwart boss Conkling insisted the Collector must be his man.

The President's nomination of Blaine's friend William Robertson for the post so shocked and dismayed the Stalwarts that both Conkling and his fellow New York Senator Thomas Platt resigned their seats on May 16. Two days later the Senate confirmed Robertson. It was thus Robertson who passed along the futile British protest against the Fenian Ram. Conkling was finished politically.

Charles Guiteau later testified that he was "inspired" to take action when Conkling was crushed. A virtual zombie, Guiteau had been for years the victim and underling of a mind-control sex cult in Oneida, N.Y,, run by the old Tory John Humphrey Noyes. Guiteau began stalking and threatening Garfield. He shot the President on July 2, when Garfield was waiting at a Washington train station with Secretaries Blaine and Lincoln. As Garfield fell, Guiteau shouted, "I am a Stalwart and Arthur is now President!"

The double murder at the outset of the Administration of the progressive Russian leader and the crusading American President, stunned the world.

Garfield held on for two months.

Ambassador Stephen Hurlbut departed the day Garfield was shot and arrived in Peru as Garfield clung to life. General Hurlbut clashed sharply with British diplomats and recognized the Presidency of Francisco García Calderón, who had been chosen by the underground Peruvian nationalist leadership.

When Garfield died in September 1881, Hurlbut asked Blaine for instructions and was told to press ahead. Blaine dispatched the *USS Alaska*, which landed a brother of President Calderón with money and instructions for Peruvian resistance fighters. Britain's Chilean proxies arrested President Calderón and took him away to Santiago.

On Nov. 29, 1881, Secretary of State Blaine called for a peace conference of all republics in the Western Hemisphere.

A number of nations had accepted the invitation when President Chester Arthur fired Blaine two weeks later. The new Secretary of State, Frederick Frelinghuysen, canceled the proposed hemispheric peace conference so as not to invite "European jealousy and ill will."

Frelinghuysen was intimate with the Rothschilds' American representative August Belmont, and was the law partner of Belmont's son Perry—a Congressman who held hearings on Blaine's "corruption." August Belmont later remarked, "the country might have been plunged into a war with Peru if poor Garfield had not been assassinated."[15]

The Aftermath

What, then, became of the American outlook that was shot down in 1881?

Years later James Blaine, again Secretary of State (1889-92), re-introduced the Pan-American policy, encompassing a bank jointly owned by the republics, and construction of a hemispheric railroad grid. Blaine's protégé, President William McKinley, was promoting this future happiness at the 1901 Pan American Exposi-

tion in Buffalo, N.Y., when an anarchist murdered him. The bullet brought in Vice President Theodore Roosevelt, who buried the United States under London-Wall Street control.

His cousin Franklin D. Roosevelt, who by the 1920s hated Teddy's British imperialism, restored the nation's honor with the Good Neighbor policy. FDR, and the later John F. Kennedy, foresaw and fought for world progress led by American science and industry. It was another double murder—of John Kennedy and his brother Robert—that has left the United States in a degraded muddle, stripped of its Revolutionary inheritance, and faced with the decision to reclaim it or die.

Americans who have repressed their consciences sometimes ask, isn't it impossible to overcome the destructive power of the imperial financiers?

The answer is no, because 19th-Century Americans brought a new and greater power into the world, giving man the tools to subdue nature and end poverty everywhere. This capability redefined the nation's mission; this power is in our hands today, and the United States is simmering with revolt.

---

15. Quoted in David Black, *The King of Fifth Avenue; The Fortunes of August Belmont* (New York: The Dial Press, 1981), p. 645.

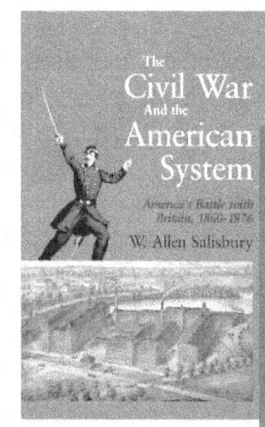

Editorial

LaRouche: Prosecute Cheney, Obama

On Dec. 30, Lyndon LaRouche joined a chorus of leading American voices demanding the criminal prosecution of former Vice President Dick Cheney, his former Legal Counsel David Addington, and others responsible for the Bush Administration's torture program. LaRouche was the first prominent American figure to demand Cheney's prosecution and impeachment, dating back to August 2002. However, at the time, corrupt leaders of both the Democratic and Republican parties agreed to take impeachment off the table.

LaRouche also demanded the impeachment and criminal prosecution of President Barack Obama for his complicity after the fact in covering up the crimes of torture committed during the previous Administration, under Cheney's personal direction. "We cannot allow these extreme Constitutional violations and violations of international law to go unpunished, if we are to survive as a nation," LaRouche asserted.

On Dec. 21, the Editorial Board of the *New York Times* sharply denounced President Obama for covering up the torture, and refusing to prosecute. The editorial demanded that Cheney, Addington, and a number of other top officials of the Bush-Cheney Administration, including officials of the Justice Department's Office of Legal Counsel who authored the "torture memo" justifying violations of international law, including the Geneva Conventions, be criminally prosecuted. Citing the unclassified 524-page Executive Summary of the Senate Select Committee on Intelligence report on the post-9/11 torture program, the *Times* editorial called these actions "depraved and illegal."

LaRouche demanded the appointment of an independent counsel with full authority to investigate and prosecute current and former top government officials who ordered these crimes against humanity, and others who actively covered up the crimes.

"As one of the surviving 16 million Americans who served in World War II and fought to defeat a Hitler Nazi regime that committed unspeakable crimes against humanity, I can speak with special authority," LaRouche stated. "Bringing these criminals to justice is the ultimate test of whether our nation has the moral fitness to survive. To tolerate and cover up such heinous actions, conducted on such a large scale, by elements of our own government, is itself a crime against our nation's principles, enshrined in our Constitution."

The very same courage, and dedication to principle, that are required for Americans to decisively reject the British Empire-style bestiality carried out in the Cheney-Bush torture program, needs to be applied to the restoration of the Constitution in other areas of policy as well, especially economics.

The United States was founded on a unique set of economic principles, defined by Alexander Hamilton, and embedded in the Constitution itself. Those principles commit our nation to the promotion of continuous scientific progress, based on fostering the creative powers of the human mind. Just as Cheney's torture program flagrantly abuses human decency, so does the current British monetarist domination of U.S. economic policy fundamentally violate our moral foundation. It is also physically ripping our nation apart.

It's time we finally mustered the courage to defeat the British Empire once and for all.